Forgive and Forget

Heartlines

Heartlines

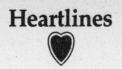

David S. Williams

Forgive and Forget

A Pan Original

First published 1985 by Pan Books Ltd,
Cavaye Place, London SW10 9PG
987654321
©David S. Williams 1985
ISBN 0 330 28952 7

Printed and bound in Great Britain by
Hazell Watson & Viney Limited,
Member of the BPCC Group,
Aylesbury, Bucks.

Chapter 1

I walked out of the main entrance to Priory Grange Comprehensive School, clutching the small computerized result slip in my hand. Though it was only ten-thirty, the August sun was warm, heralding another sizzling summer day. I shook my head with incredulity and glanced again at the strip of paper to make sure I'd read it correctly. There, printed in small regular letters, were my 'O'-level results. I felt elation bubble up inside me, washing away my disbelief, and making me feel light-headed.

Then someone called my name, and turning, I saw Simon Fenton running across the yard. I'd been so excited that I'd forgotten to wait for him while he went to collect his own results.

Just over six feet tall, with fair wavy hair that flopped untidily over a broad tanned forehead, he was one of the best-looking guys in the fifth form.

'Wait for me, Claire,' he yelled and seconds later, came to a halt beside me. 'Well . . . how did you do?'

I shook my head again. 'Would you believe it? I got eight . . . all eight . . . three 'A's, three 'B's and two 'C's. Honestly, I never expected to do so well . . . ' Instantly, I felt guilty because I hadn't asked how he'd done. 'And you? How did you do?'

He grinned and shrugged his shoulders. 'Not as well

as you . . . but I'm satisfied. Seven 'O's and a C.S.E. in History . . . '

'Oh, I'm sorry . . . about the History.'

'No need to be. I don't really need History for what I've got in mind. And anyway, I did get four 'B's and three 'C's . . . so I don't consider I've done so badly . . . '

I felt pleasure surge inside me. 'That's fantastic, Simon. It really is.'

He flicked back the lock of straying hair. 'So? What are we going to do now?'

'Well . . . ' I began. 'I promised to meet Dawn at Raffles.'

Raffles was the local coffee shop, and Dawn was my best friend. Only the night before she'd confessed she was scared of collecting her results.

When I told Simon of her fears, he frowned and shook his head. 'I don't know what she's worried about. I mean . . . it's not as if she's stupid or anything.'

'I know. But she gets so nervous when she sits her exams, it's a wonder she can write anything at all.'

Simon looked down at me and gave a quick shrug of his broad shoulders. 'Well . . . let's go and see her, shall we?'

Raffles was less than half a mile from the school and as soon as I entered the modern restaurant with its aroma of freshly-ground coffee, I saw Dawn sitting near one of the huge plate-glass windows. With her fine brown hair straggling over her eyes, she was staring gloomily into the street. And yet I knew she wasn't watching the traffic that trundled past.

While Simon went to get the coffees, I weaved through the cluster of tables towards her. She looked up, and when I sat opposite and asked the inevitable question, she gave a brief twisted smile.

'I got five . . . three 'O'-levels and two C.S.E.s,' she said with a woeful sigh.

'But that's not bad, Dawn.' I did my best to sound encouraging, without being patronizing. 'After all, last night you didn't think you'd get any.'

She gave me another smile, a slightly happier one this time. 'I suppose you're right. Anyway . . . ' She seemed to brighten up as a thought occurred to her. ' . . . at least I've got the qualifications for getting into that pre-nursing course at the Tech. They did say they'd accept me if I got 'O'-levels in English and Maths.'

'Which you've got,' I pointed out.

By the time Simon arrived with the coffees, she had cheered up, and the fact that we'd both done much better than she had didn't seem to affect her at all. Except to make her glad for us.

'It looks like we've all got something to celebrate,' Simon said. 'What about going out tonight? Somewhere special.'

I nodded in agreement. 'Sounds great to me. Where do you suggest?'

'What about the Swan Inn? They serve fantastic bar meals. And we could sit outside . . . on those picnic benches.'

My stomach tightened with excitement. I turned to Dawn. 'What about you? Do you think Julian would come?'

Julian was Dawn's steady, who worked in one of the banks in the High Street.

'I'm sure he would,' she replied. 'As a matter of fact, he did promise to take me out tonight. To drown my sorrows if there was nothing to celebrate.'

'That's fixed then.' Simon took a sip of his coffee. 'We meet at the Swan . . . eight o'clock . . . and the first ones there grab a table.'

A quarter of an hour later we were walking to the crossroads in the centre of town where the almost continuous traffic weaved around the medieval stone cross, its carving blunted by time and grimy with smoke. We paused for a minute or so. Dawn agreed to call round that afternoon while Simon declared mysteriously that he had something important to do. Then we went our separate ways.

Remembering that I'd promised to let my mother know my results, I hurried down a side street to her boutique, tucked between a high class delicatessen and a jeweller's. With its low door and bow window, it reminded me of something out of Dickens.

Pressing down the old-fashioned latch, I opened the door to the gentle tinkling of a bell and stepped into a large room. At the far end was a counter with a door leading to the store room at one side, and two curtained cubicles on the other. In the centre were circular chrome stands packed with clothes of all descriptions. The lighting was bright and subdued music played one of the latest ballads.

I had hardly entered before my mother came rushing towards me. 'Claire. Where on earth have you been? You promised to come and tell me how you've done . . . '

'I'm sorry, Mum. Simon and I went for a coffee.'

'Coffee. You went for a coffee while I was going through all sorts of agony . . . thinking all sorts of things . . . ' Mum was being her usual melodramatic self, and though I took after her artistically, I had my father's calm logical ways. 'Well . . . aren't you going to tell me the good news . . . ?' She hesitated and put a hand to her lips. 'Don't tell me it's bad.'

I grinned and handed her the result slip. She glanced at it and a smile of sheer delight lit up her face. 'But this is marvellous, darling . . . simply marvellous . . . but then . . . ' she put on that sloppy mumsy voice she sometimes used in the house. 'I always knew my baby was clever . . . '

Her words horrified me. 'Mum! Stop it!' I whispered, feeling myself go hot all over as I glanced over my shoulder and saw the amused looks in the eyes of the four or five people there.

Not that my plea had any effect.

'But it's true,' she said, blithely ignoring the fact that she'd just embarrassed me. 'I always knew you could do it.' Then she hurried to the back of the shop.

'Must phone your father,' she called over her shoulder. 'He'll be dying to hear how well you've done.'

While she was dialling, I ambled round inspecting the racks, my body swaying to the gentle rhythm of the music.

A minute or two later Mrs Metcalfe, my mother's assistant, who had just finished serving, came over.

'Congratulations, Claire. Your mother's just told me the good news.'

Though Mrs Metcalfe was a few years older than my mother, she was dressed in a dark skirt and white blouse which accentuated her youthful figure. And since her hair was still dark she gave the impression of being at least ten years younger.

'Have you decided what you're going to do now?' she asked.

I nodded. 'Go into the sixth form. Take my 'A'-levels and go to university . . . I hope . . . '

She squeezed my arm. 'Very wise too. These days everybody's going to need the best qualifications possible if they're going to get a good job . . . '

At that moment, my mother returned looking very annoyed.

'Honestly. Your father is one of the most trying men I've ever met. Whenever I want to get in touch with him, he's in some meeting or other. And he knew I was going to phone him this morning . . . ' Then the look of annoyance faded. 'Oh, never mind. I've left word he's to call me back. And now . . . ' She gave me an excited hug. 'I'm going to let you choose anything you want . . . and afterwards we're going to lunch'.

I gave a gasp of pleasure. 'Honestly? Anything?'

'Of course!' she replied, her eyes moist with pride. 'That's what I said, didn't I?'

'Oh Mum!' It was my turn to hug her. 'I don't know what to say.'

I spent almost an hour searching the rails and trying on so many things that I was more undecided than when I first began. Eventually, however, I chose a nobbly light-green sweater with latticed sleeves and a deep V-back as well as a pair of cream linen trousers, both of which fitted perfectly.

My mother nodded with approval as I paraded in front of her. 'You look really nice,' she said. 'Now you have something really special to wear tonight.'

Then she took me to a small Italian restaurant in the next street where she treated me to my favourite meal, so that it was almost two o'clock by the time I arrived home.

Curiously, I felt quite deflated and the sense of anticlimax which swept over me was so strong that I was glad when Dawn arrived. We lay on sun loungers on the patio, sipping long cool glasses of iced lemonade and talking drowsily to each other. My eyes were shut behind darkly tinted glasses and I could feel the sun hot on my body when Dawn said suddenly, 'I bet Simon didn't like it this morning.'

'Didn't like what?' I could hear the soporific buzz of a bee about my head.

'Didn't like you doing better than him.'

I opened one eye and squinted at her. 'That's a stupid thing to say.'

'Is it?' Dawn rolled over on her side. 'I know he's your fella, Claire. But even you must admit, he thinks he's God's gift to mankind.'

This time I sat bolt upright. ' . . . and *that*'s a horrible thing to say.'

'I'm sorry, Claire. I don't mean to be unkind . . . but it's the truth, isn't it? He likes to be the centre of attention. He doesn't like anyone doing better than him . . . even you.'

I opened my mouth to say something but couldn't think of anything vicious enough.

'Of course he is rather dishy,' she went on. 'His father's absolutely loaded with money . . . he can be great fun . . . and all the girls are crazy about him. So . . . ' She gave a sigh. 'I suppose he's got every right to be big-headed.'

I bristled with indignation. 'Thank you very much, Dawn Sutton,' I said with an icy smile. 'But you can't fool me. You're just plain jealous.'

She gave a mischievous giggle. 'Perhaps you're right. Better watch I don't pinch him off you then.'

I lay back, pretending to be unconcerned. 'You

could try. But I wouldn't fancy your chances,' I replied.

But inside I was seething. How dare she say such things about Simon! Perhaps he *was* the best-looking guy around! Perhaps all the girls *were* crazy about him! Perhaps he *did* like to be the centre of attention! Who wouldn't?

I glanced at Dawn basking in the sun with her eyes shut, a smile of sheer devilment on her face. I picked up my glass of iced lemonade and felt its chill numb my fingers. It was half-way to my lips when I paused. Shall I? I thought. Why not! She deserves it. I leaned across and calmly tipped it over her bare midriff.

The resulting scream of anguish gave me the most malicious sense of satisfaction.

My mother arrived home shortly before six annoyed that my father hadn't phoned back. I frowned, perplexed as well as disappointed. I had been longing all day for him to hear the news, and though he was often too busy to talk to us at work, it was nevertheless unusual for him to be at a meeting for so long.

'Never mind, Mum,' I said, consoling her. 'I'm sure it must be something important to keep him away from a phone for so long.'

My mother wasn't so easily placated. 'I hope you're right,' she muttered darkly. 'Because he's going to know all about it when he gets home . . . and I don't just mean your results . . . '

We waited another half-hour before deciding to have dinner without him, but when Simon arrived to pick me up and Dad still hadn't arrived Mum was absolutely livid. Though she did her best to hide it.

'You go and enjoy yourself,' she said, squeezing my arm. 'You've deserved it . . . '

As soon as I left the house, I took Mum's advice and

thrust the niggling worry about my father right out of my mind. Simon and I walked hand-in-hand down the tree-lined streets to the river that flowed through the centre of town.

There was magic in the air that night. We sauntered slowly along the old tow-path for about half a mile. The sun had already set and in the growing dusk I could hear the sound of the river slapping against the bank. Above it, swallows dipped and darted across the surface, their wings flicking the water and filling the air with their whirring.

Soon we arrived at the Swan and, as we entered the beer garden, Julian stood up and waved. Now that dusk had finally fallen, two spotlights had been switched on, bathing the thatched roof of the old inn in their beams while a string of fairy lights, red, yellow, green and blue, ringed the garden, festooning the trees that lined the river bank, completing the air of unreality that had enveloped me all that day.

It really was a fantastic night. The boys ordered the meals and the drinks and as we sat there laughing together, I glanced round at the three closest friends I'd ever had and wished with all my heart that it would never end. Not just the night. I wanted our friendship to last for ever. But then I realized it couldn't be.

'Are you aware,' I said, with a slight sinking feeling deep in my stomach, 'that there'll only be two of us left at school next term?' I turned to Dawn. 'Julian's already left . . . you'll be going to the Tech. There'll just be me and Simon . . . it's going to be strange without you . . . '

'Wrong!' It was Simon who spoke and his word made us all turn. 'There'll only be you, Claire.'

I felt a sudden tightening in my throat. 'Only me?

What do you mean?'

'What I say. I'm not returning to school.'

'But you said if you had the right result, you'd be going into the Sixth Form too.'

'No I didn't. I only said I might . . . Now I've decided to do something quite different.'

Julian glanced at Dawn, then at me. 'Like what?'

'Like joining the Air Force.'

'The Air Force!' Our three voices came out in a chorus.

Simon put a hand into his pocket and brought out a small booklet and handed it to me.

'That's where I went this morning . . . after I left you . . . to the Recruiting Office in the High Street . . . '

I wasn't really listening. In the glimmer of light from the coloured bulb above my head, I was peering at the booklet. In the centre were printed the words Commissions as Aircrew Officers in the Royal Air Force, and above them was the R.A.F. crest.

My mind was spinning. All this wasn't happening, I tried to tell myself.

'You know I've always been keen on flying,' I heard him say as though from a distance. 'So . . . like I said, I went to this Recruitment Office and made some inquiries. Anyway to cut a long story short, they told me I had the right qualifications . . . just the sort of guy they were looking for . . . '

The pride in his voice – which bordered upon conceit – made me think of what Dawn had said that afternoon.

'Must have been blind,' said Julian jokingly.

'As thick as two short planks,' added Dawn.

I said nothing. I just sat there feeling sick.

'When are you going?' I said at last, my voice a mere

croak as I tried to hide my disappointment.

'Depends if they accept me,' he said, totally oblivious of the way I was feeling. 'Anyway, it won't be for a long time yet . . . not until the New Year.'

'The New Year?' I echoed. 'But that's only four months away.'

'Yeah. I know. But I've got lots of things to do before then. I have to wait to see if they accept my application . . . then if they do, I'll have to go to Biggin Hill for aptitude tests and things like that. And if everything's all right, they'll let me join up when I'm seventeen and a half.'

I added up quickly. Simon would be seventeen on the third of September. He'd be seventeen and a half on the third of March. That meant in just over six months, he'd be leaving me.

It was Dawn who eventually broke the silence. 'Great. That leaves just three of us . . . '

Julian shook his head. 'No. It leaves two . . . '

We turned in amazement.

'I wasn't going to tell you right now,' he continued. 'But I'm being transferred . . . to a branch in Chelmsford.'

I'd never seen Dawn look so unhappy in my whole life. 'Fantastic!' Her voice held more than a mere trace of bitterness. 'Looks like the gang is splitting up, doesn't it?'

In a few brief moments, my whole life had been turned upside down, and the magic of the evening cruelly dispelled. With both Simon and Julian away, what on earth were Dawn and I going to do, I wondered bitterly. Twiddle our thumbs all day?'

And that was before I heard the news that awaited me at home!

Chapter 2

I felt miserable all the way home – even after Simon kissed me good-night. I closed the front door behind me to the sound of raised voices coming from the living-room; my mother's shrill tone masked by the deeper growl of my father's voice. Which was unusual. My father rarely lost his temper, and though my mother would nag at times and moan about how tired she was after standing all day, my father always kept his cool. But now I could hear both his anger and frustration.

'How the hell can you blame me, Vanessa? Anyone would swear that I actually wanted to be transferred.'

'I wouldn't put that past you.'

'That's unfair. You know I wouldn't uproot Claire. Not now when she's doing so well . . . '

There was a momentary lull and as I stood in the gloom of the hall, I could imagine my mother taking a deep breath as she realized she'd gone too far.

'All right. I'm sorry. But there isn't just Claire. There's Robert too . . . '

'Robert's all right. He's at university . . . '

'But it's still his home, Derrick. He comes home at the end of every term . . . as well as the occasional weekend.'

There was contempt in my father's voice now. 'He'll still be able to come home . . . wherever we live . . . '

There was another lull. Then my mother went on. 'What about me? Don't I count? What about my business?'

'Ah! Now we're coming to the heart of the matter.' I'd never heard my father so bitter. 'That's what's bugging you.'

That made my mother blow her top. 'Now who's being unfair? Of course the business matters to me. It's taken ten years to build up . . . and now it's really doing well, you're asking me to throw it all away.'

I'd heard enough to know that something very serious was happening. I thrust open the door and marched into the living-room. Dad was standing near the fire, his elbow resting on the mantelpiece, while my mother paced the room, her arms hugging her body the way she did whenever she was in a temper.

'Claire!' Guilt chased astonishment from her face. 'I didn't hear you come in. How long have you been there?'

I looked from one to the other. 'Long enough!' I muttered accusingly.

Dad was the first to recover. He shot my mother a warning glance and came towards me, smiling and pretending that everything was all right.

'Hey. You've done well, I hear . . . '

I stepped back, ignoring his congratulations. 'I'd like to know what's going on, please?' I insisted quietly.

My mother gave a deep sigh and glanced coldly at my father. 'I think you'd better tell her, Derrick. She's old enough now to be told the truth . . . especially as she's the one who's going to be most affected . . . '

The barb wasn't lost on my father. If he didn't actually wince, he frowned and looked down at the floor in confusion.

For a moment he couldn't speak.

'I'll tell her if you like.' She obviously wasn't going to let him off the hook.

My father looked up, anger steeling his eyes. 'No thanks. I'm quite capable . . . '

I know that all parents quarrel at times, and mine were no exception, but this was far worse than anything I'd ever experienced. But when he turned to me, the anger had melted away.

'You'd better sit down,' he said with a tight smile. 'I'll try and explain.'

My mother turned abruptly and walked into the kitchen. As I perched on the edge of an armchair, Dad went back to his favourite place by the fire, adopting his usual stance whenever he had something important to say. In the brief silence I heard traffic lumbering along the road.

'It's like this, Claire. For some time now, there's been a rumour at work about a take-over bid. I didn't mention it earlier because . . . well, I didn't want to worry you . . . and besides it could have been just that . . . a rumour . . . '

I glanced up. 'But it wasn't?'

'No.' He shook his head slowly. 'I'm afraid it wasn't. This morning, I was called into a series of meetings and discussions which lasted until early this evening. Which is why I couldn't get in touch with you.'

He gave me an apologetic smile before going on. 'Anyway, to cut a long story short, we were all informed that a take-over had actually occurred . . . and that there were going to be changes . . . '

As I listened to him, I felt that all this wasn't happening. That I was taking part in some horrible dream. Just as I had back at the Swan.

'Changes?' I said. 'What changes?'

'Well . . . to begin with . . . a lot of people have lost their jobs . . . '

'You as well?'

'No. . . .not me . . . at least . . . ' He paused as though struggling to find the right words. 'I suppose in a way I have. I've lost the job I'm doing now. But they've offered me another one instead.' He levered himself off the mantelpiece and looked down at me. 'That's what all the trouble is about . . . '

I didn't say anything. I just sat there biting my lip. Then he delivered his bombshell.

'You see . . . the job they've offered me is in Wales.'

'Wales?' I echoed. All I could remember about Wales from my geography lessons was that it was mountainous, dotted with coal mines – and that it rained a lot. 'But I don't want to live there . . . I want to stay here . . . with my friends.'

He shook his head and sighed. 'I'm afraid we don't have much choice, Claire.'

Anger bubbled up inside me and my eyes began to water. 'I don't care . . . ' I stood up defiantly. 'I won't go and live there. Do you hear? I won't . . . '

At that moment, my mother returned with a tray. 'Have you told her everything?'

I felt my heart go cold. 'Everything?'

'Yes. Has your father told you when we have to leave?' It was always 'your father' when she was angry.

I glanced at him and he shook his head. Then my mother went on. 'He starts there next week. Though how he expects us to go with him at a moment's notice, I don't know.'

I was shattered. 'But that means I won't be going back at all to Priory Grange . . . '

'That's right . . . '

I turned to my father. 'Oh, Dad. Must we go? Surely you could find another job . . . around here if not in London . . . '

He shook his head gravely. 'I only wish I could, Claire. But I'm forty-eight. I doubt if any other firm would take me on. Believe me, I'm lucky that I'm being transferred. Some men didn't get the choice . . . '

I was only half-listening. I was thinking of Simon, Dawn, Julian and all the other friends I'd made over the years. Now I was going to leave them. Not see them at weekends even – let alone at holidays.

My mother offered me a coffee but I didn't take it. All I could do was shake my head as tears welled up in my eyes. Then I turned and fled upstairs, flinging myself on to my bed and crying until my chest ached and my heart felt as though it had been broken into millions of little pieces.

It was several minutes before my mother came up and sat on the edge of my bed. I couldn't look at her; I just buried my face in my pillow as I felt her hand on my shoulder.

'Oh, Claire!' she sighed. 'I do know how you feel . . . and I hate to see you crying like this, but . . . Oh, I could kill your father sometimes . . . ' Then she paused and her resentment seemed to melt away. 'But it's not his fault . . . it's not as if he's done it on purpose . . . '

I turned on to my back and wiped my nose with the tissue she offered.

'Do we really have to go?' I asked desperately. 'Couldn't we stay here? Dad could always travel home at weekends, couldn't he?'

She frowned. 'That's expecting rather a lot of him. It's over a hundred miles . . . each way.'

'I don't mean all the time . . . only until he found a better job.'

'I don't think that's very likely, darling.' She smiled indulgently and shook her head. 'Your father's right, he'd never get a better offer . . . '

'Then couldn't I stay here . . . while you and dad go to Wales?'

There was shock as well as surprise in her eyes. 'Don't be ridiculous, Claire. Where on earth would you stay?'

I thought frantically. 'With Dawn. I'm sure Mrs Sutton wouldn't mind.'

'No.'

'But Mum . . . ' I wailed.

'Claire. I said no.' She rose to her feet and her attitude told me that the discussion was at an end.

'We're a family, Claire. And as a family we must stick together.' She tucked my duvet round my shoulders. 'I think you ought to go to sleep now. I have the feeling that the next few weeks are going to be absolutely horrendous. . . '

Sleep, of course, was impossible, especially when my father popped in as he went to bed.

'I'm sorry about all this, Claire. Honestly, I am, but . . . ' He shrugged his shoulders helplessly, and for a brief moment, I was sorry for him. 'I'm sure it won't be as bad as you think.'

'Won't it?'

He squeezed my hand. 'No. it won't. It's not far from Swansea . . . A small town called Pencarnog.'

'Pen what?'

He spelt it out for me, syllable by syllable. 'Pen – car – nog.'

I was far from impressed. 'It sounds terrible.'

But Dad smiled. 'I'm sure you'll like Swansea. They tell me it's quite a nice city . . . and as for Pencarnog . . . well, it's right out in the country . . . '

'We're in the country here,' I reminded him.

'And yet the sea's not that far away . . . only twenty miles . . . ' He seemed determined to have the last word. But he was underestimating me: I could be as determined as my mother when I wanted to be.

'Look, Dad,' I said, as patiently as I could. 'It really is no use trying to make me change my mind. I like living here. I shall never like living in Pencarnog or whatever it's called. I mean it. Never.'

And that, as far as I was concerned, was that.

I awoke late next morning. Getting to sleep hadn't been easy, and as I lay in the dark I began to wish that I hadn't been so abrupt with my father. But eventually I dozed off, emerging occasionally from my troubled dreams to find that reality was much worse. I glanced at the clock on my bedside cabinet. It was a quarter to ten and already, the sunlight streaming through the thin summer curtain told me that it was going to be another hot day. Both Mum and Dad had left for work, but I knew from the movement coming from the kitchen that Robert had already risen. Which surprised me. He was normally the last home at night, as well as the last to get up next morning.

Putting on dressing gown and slippers, I ventured downstairs and found my elder brother buttering some toast he'd just cremated. Tall, with fair curly hair, he was four or five inches taller than my father, as well as being more solidly built. And yet looking at him, I realized that Dad must have looked remarkably like Robert when he was younger. But unlike my father, he had a small scar over his left eye – the souvenir of a slight accident on the Rugby field.

He looked up, took a bite of the burnt offering and grinned. 'Hi, menace,' he said. 'Did you hear last night's exciting news?'

I slumped on to a chair and rolled my eyes. 'Didn't I! I've been having nightmares about it.' I picked up a slice of his toast and nibbled it. It was hard, dry and bitter. I wrinkled my nose with distaste. 'I mean . . . Dad expects me to go and live in Wales . . . just like that . . . he didn't even ask my opinion.'

'No one asked him either.' Robert pointed out.

'I know,' I admitted gloomily 'But I don't want to live in Wales. I know I'll just hate it . . . '

'You surprise me. I'd have thought you'd have found the prospect exciting.'

I looked at him with contempt. 'Oh, Robert. Don't be so stupid. What could be exciting about living in a grotty place like Pen . . . ' I tried to remember how to pronounce the name.

'Pencarnog,' Robert prompted me. 'Anyway, you don't know that it is grotty . . . it could be great . . . '

I just scowled at him as he went on.

'As for the Welsh, I've always found them very friendly.'

'Oh you would.' Robert played rugby for his university and I'd often heard him speak of his Welsh friends.

'But it's true,' he protested. 'I'm sure you'll enjoy making new friends when you get there.'

'That's just it.' I leaned over the table. 'I don't want to make new friends. I'm happy with the ones I've got.'

Robert's eyes were unusually serious. 'Now look, Claire. You're going to have to make new friends some time. In two years you'll be going to university . . . '

'So?'

'It's not likely that anyone at Priory Grange will land up in the same college, is it? You'll have to make new friends then.' He got up and poured two cups of coffee. 'Look at me. All the mates I had at school, they're not around any longer. Do you know? I actually feel lonely when I come home.'

His words startled me. 'Honestly?'

'Of course.' He placed a mug in front of me. 'Why do you think I stay with my university friends so often? Because I haven't got any around here any more. That's why.'

I hadn't thought of Robert being lonely before. 'But you always have plenty of girlfriends when you're home,' I pointed out sullenly.

'That's true. But they're all new ones.' He emphasized the word 'new' and grinned. 'Which explains why I have so many.'

'Huh! Big-head.' I retorted. 'I really don't know what they see in you.'

That wasn't quite true. Robert was good-looking in an ugly sort of way and he often had the girls running after him. I'd even noticed that some of the girls at school went misty-eyed whenever they saw him.

'And there's another thing,' he continued. 'In two years' time when I graduate, I'm going to lose my present friends and make new ones. I know that right now. I have to accept it . . . just as you have to.'

His words depressed me and I took a sip of my coffee. Robert stirred his slowly.

'At least, you must admit that Dad's firm have been pretty decent to him.'

I looked up, surprised and angry. 'You call it

decent . . . after all the years he's worked for them . . . to be . . . to be sent to some backwater . . . '

He shook his head. 'I don't think you understand. If they didn't think highly of him, they wouldn't have offered him this job. You do realize they're making him manager of a factory, don't you?'

I didn't, but I wasn't going to tell him so.

'And they really are making things easy for him.'

'Easy? How?'

'They've booked him into a first-class hotel . . . at their expense . . . as well as giving him a bridging loan to buy another house . . . besides making sure he's not out of pocket. So . . . he doesn't have to worry about the financial side of things.' He sipped his coffee and looked across the table at me. 'But he was worried sick when I got home last night . . . and I have a suspicion it was over you.'

I thought about the way I'd spoken to him and felt guilt churn deep inside me.

'You're right,' I confessed. 'I was pretty beastly to him. I told him how I felt . . . I didn't consider his feelings at all.'

I broke off and bit my lip as tears of remorse began to sting my eyes. Robert tousled my hair.

'Hey. Come on. I'm sure Dad understands you didn't mean to be so blunt . . . You were upset.'

I looked up and sighed. 'Do you think I ought to apologize?'

Robert smiled. 'Just try being sympathetic; that'll be enough . . . '

But I still didn't want to leave and told him so.

'Not now, perhaps,' he said. 'But when you get used to the idea, who knows? Anyway, you won't be leaving for several weeks, will you?'

But he was wrong.

On the weekend my father left, Mum insisted on going with him — just to pay a flying visit — and when she returned, her previous antagonism had vanished.

'Pencarnog is a lovely town,' she enthused. 'It's so quaint. Not at all what I expected. And the people are so friendly. And . . . listen both of you . . . ' Robert looked up from his meal, ' . . . we've found the house we want . . . '

'So soon,' Robert exclaimed.

Mum nodded. 'It's about a mile outside town . . . it has a large garden, and . . . this is the most important thing, it's empty. We could move in a few weeks . . . provided the owners agree.'

'What about your boutique?' I muttered, determined somehow to curb her enthusiasm.

She smiled indulgently. 'Don't worry about that, my love. We'll work something out in time.'

After that, events moved quickly. Dad phoned next day to say that he'd put a deposit on the house. On Friday, we heard that it might be possible to move in soon; perhaps within a week. His solicitor was contacting the owners that day. And that evening he phoned to tell us to start packing.

And exactly a week later, the furniture had been carried aboard the removal van, Robert had returned early to university, I'd said goodbye to Simon, Dawn and Julian, and Mum and I were tucked up for the night in a local hotel.

The next morning we left for Wales.

Chapter 3

We had breakfast early that morning and shortly before nine drove to Mum's boutique where she had a last word with Mrs Metcalfe. Then, to my horror, she returned to Hilltop Close so that she could make sure that all was well, though I knew that like me she really didn't want to leave.

I refused to go back into the house with her – nothing could have induced me to relive the agony of leaving – so I stayed in the car, hunched in the front seat, wishing that she would hurry up. Of course, two or three of our neighbours came out and delayed us for a few minutes, but eventually Mum returned to the car, her eyes large and liquid.

'Well . . . we'd better get on our way, I suppose . . .' Her voice was artificially bright though she couldn't quite control the slight quiver in it. 'Your father will be wondering where we've got to.'

I didn't say a word. I didn't even point out that it was she who had delayed us. I just sank deeper into my seat and shut my eyes tightly, determined not to look back at the house I had grown to love so much. I felt tears squeeze past my eyelids, and turning my head away from my mother, didn't open them until we were clear of the town and the M4 motorway was just a mile away.

We hardly spoke, but after about an hour, my mother glanced at me.

'Would you like to stop at the service area on the Severn Bridge?' she asked. 'We could have some coffee.'

I shrugged my shoulders. 'If you like,' I muttered ungraciously.

'I think we'd better,' she went on. 'Then we won't have to stop until we reach Pencarnog.'

The mere mention of the place made my stomach twist, and thankfully, Mum, who must have realized how I was feeling, didn't pursue the matter further. We drove into the car park and then made our way back to the large building we had just passed. We mounted the stairs, and entered the cafeteria on the first floor.

'If you sit at one of the tables,' she said, picking up a brown plastic tray. 'I'll get the coffees.'

I walked down a small flight of steps and weaved my way to a table facing the river. I gazed down into the swirling waters of the Severn, thick and brown and menacing, and then at the bridge: two huge pillars, one on each side of the river, with the road, looking deceptively frail and insecure, suspended from cables. In the distance were the hills of Wales, dark with foreboding, even though the day was sunny.

Mum joined me presently and placed a coffee and a slice of Black Forest gateau in front of me. 'I thought you might like it,' she explained, 'Seeing it's your favourite.'

I smiled weakly at her. She was trying anxiously to please me, to compensate for what was happening, and normally I would have been delighted. I honestly didn't know whether or not I could eat it, but to refuse would have been mean and churlish. So I dutifully spooned my way through it even though it tasted like sawdust.

As I did so, I thought of Simon and wondered what he was doing at that moment. And then I had one of the biggest shocks of my life. I couldn't remember him; I couldn't recall what he looked like. It was as though he had gone out of my mind completely. I felt my whole body shake as my eyes began to mist up.

'What is it, Claire?' my mother asked anxiously. 'Is anything wrong?'

'No. Everything's all right.' I replied, unable to keep the bitterness out of my voice. 'Why shouldn't it be.'

When we left, I asked if I could lie down on the back seat. I told my mother I wasn't feeling very well though really I just wanted to close my eyes and get out of my misery. I looked up at the twin towers of the bridge, at the flickering lines of vertical cables, and closed my eyes tightly. It was as though I was crossing into another world. Desperately, I willed his image back, and as Simon's familiar face appeared in my mind, I gave a long contented sigh of relief and slid gently into a dream where I was back home, waiting for him to call round.

All too soon, I felt a hand shake my shoulder. 'Come on, sleepy head.' Mum's voice gently eased me out of my slumber. 'We're almost there.'

I sat up and rubbed my eyes. We had left the motorway and were parked in a lay-by at the top of a low hill.

'There it is,' she said, pointing to a cluster of buildings about a mile or so away. 'Pencarnog.'

It was a small town perched on the bank of a river that looped through a surprisingly wide valley. Behind it were hills which rose steeply; bare hills which receded into a purple distance. Yet in spite of their starkness, they possessed a wild attractive beauty.

'What do you think of it?' she asked.

I shrugged my shoulders. It certainly lacked the lushness of home, and the river which gleamed in the afternoon sun was nowhere near as wide.

'It's different,' I admitted begrudgingly, joining her in the front.

'That's one way of putting it.' She put her hand on my knee. 'I'm sure you'll like it here . . . when you get used to it. So please, Claire . . . for your father's sake . . . give it a chance . . . ' She switched on the engine. 'And now we'd better see how your father's managed with the furniture.'

A few minutes later, I got my first close look at Percarnog. Two main roads crossed at the traffic lights in the centre and most of the houses, which had long ago been converted into shops, were built of dressed local stone, dark grey like the surrounding hills, though here and there were large modern stores with bright exteriors.

We turned left at the crossroads, circled the public park with its neat flower beds and paths which radiated from a bandstand in the middle and drove up a gently sloping road lined with mature trees that followed the curve of the river. Then, Mum gave an excited cry. 'Here we are, Claire. Home!'

I felt again that now familiar sinking feeling in the pit of my stomach. Home? I thought. How could this place ever be home for me? Home was where Simon and all the others were.

But a surprise awaited me. She pulled into a gravelled drive that circled a lawn and came to a halt outside the front door of a house that was almost twice the size of the one at Hilltop Close. Built of the same material as the other houses in the street, it had, however, been cleaned recently so that the stone now glowed warmly in the afternoon sun. There was a glassed-in porch made of mahogany and to the side of it, a deep purple clematis scrambled up to the bedroom windows.

Mum tooted the horn and seconds later, Dad came rushing out. Dressed in jeans and a navy-blue polo-necked sweater, its sleeves rolled up over his strong arms, he looked older and leaner than I remembered.

But that's ridiculous, I thought; he's only been away a few weeks. He couldn't possibly have altered so much in such a short time. But seeing him standing there, grinning with pleasure, made me realize suddenly just how much I had missed him.

I tumbled out of the car and rushed into his outstretched arms. With a laugh, he spun me round so fast that the whole world whirled around me and I felt quite giddy.

He stood back and looked at me closely. 'Hey! I didn't realize just how pretty you were. I reckon the boys around here are going to phone up all hours when they find out . . . '

I blushed with a mixture of pride and embarrassment. 'Oh, Dad. I wish you wouldn't say things like that.'

Mum joined us. He gave her a kiss, put his arms around our shoulders and faced the house. 'Well, Claire. What do you think of it?'

I had to tell him the truth. 'It's . . . it's beautiful, Dad. It really is . . . '

'I told you it was, didn't I?' Mum's voice held a hint of rebuke. 'But of course you wouldn't believe me.'

'I'm sorry, Mum I didn't mean it. Honestly.'

She broke into a smile. 'I know. You may find this

hard to believe, my girl, but I was young once myself . . . and now . . . ' She walked to the porch. ' . . . you must see what it's like inside.'

She led the way into a large hall. Above the front door was a tall stained-glass window and the sunlight streaming through it made patterns on the highly polished wood floor. To the right was a wide staircase leading up to a galleried landing. There were four rooms on the ground floor; a lounge, a study which Dad had already commandeered for himself, a kitchen which had been enlarged and modernized, and finally a room which my father laughingly referred to as the 'great hall'.

Facing west, it travelled the depth of the house from front to back. It had five large arched windows, the centre one of which had been converted into a French window and opened on to a patio.

'This is my favourite room,' he announced proudly, walking to the centre and looking around at the panelled walls which gleamed warmly. 'Just the place for a party. Do you know, I reckon we could get fifty of your friends in here and still have plenty of room . . . '

'Except I haven't got any friends,' I pointed out rather ungraciously.

His eyes went grave and immediately I wished I hadn't uttered the words. 'Give yourself time, Claire,' he said. 'In a couple of weeks you'll have plenty, I'm sure . . . '

Mum, who had left us alone to make an inspection of the house returned. 'I must say, you've been working hard, Derrick. Everything's just as I wanted it.'

'There's a lot more to be done yet.'

'I know. But you must have started work exceptionally early this morning to get so much done.'

He put his arm around her. 'That's because I didn't want you moaning. I've got enough problems on my plate as it is ... at work ... '

She arched her eyebrows. 'Don't tell me they're antagonistic.'

Dad grinned and shook his head. 'Not really. Let's just say they're suspicous of the new manager ... '

'The new broom sweeping clean?'

'Something like that. Anyhow, I'm lucky in my sales director. He's a real gem ... Geoff Evans. As a matter of fact, he came round this morning to give me a hand ... and to invite us to his place for dinner tonight.'

'That's kind of him. Now we'll only need a snack for lunch.' She dug him playfully in the ribs. 'Which will give you more time to get all the other jobs done, I see you managed to do it in time ... ' she added mysteriously.

I had the sudden feeling that this was something to do with me. 'Do what?' I asked.

Dad grinned. 'If you really want to know,' he said. 'You'd better see your bedroom.'

It was a huge room situated at the rear of the house. There were two large windows, one in each of the outer walls, and beneath each were cushioned window seats. Along another wall were fitted wardrobes with my bed lodged between them, while in the corner was my writing desk complete with bookshelves. A new carpet had also been laid. But what impressed me most was that it was the only room in the house that had been redecorated with the wallpaper matching the brand-new quilt and curtains.

'Well? What do you think of it?' Dad had been

watching me anxiously.

'Oh, Dad. It's fantastic.' My voice caught in my throat. 'But you shouldn't have done it. You must have had much more important things to do . . .'

'Nonsense. It was the least I could have done.' He put his arm round my shoulder and gave me a quick hug. 'Anyway, I didn't do it myself. I had the decorators in . . .'

Then Mum pointed out the settee which I hadn't noticed behind the door. Beside it was my stereo system. 'We thought it would be more comfortable,' she explained, 'especially when you ask your friends home . . .'

They had both gone out of their way to make sure I liked my new home, and it made me feel a little guilty to think that I must have made life rather difficult for them.

'It's lovely, Mum.' I said. 'It'll be like having my own bed-sit.' I gave her a kiss and the smile she returned me made me feel much happier. Indeed, I was surprised by the elation inside me which was already dispelling the air of depression and futility in which I'd been living for so long.

I spent the next half hour sorting out my clothes and then sat on the window seat gazing out at the garden. In the middle of a wide lawn was a gnarled apple tree, obviously the remnant of an orchard, and about a hundred yards away, shielded from the house by a belt of conifers, was the river which glinted in the after-noon sun.

Presently, my mother called, asking me to come down to lunch. My father had arrived back from the local take-away and only when the aroma of sweet and sour chicken and fried rice wafted up the stairs did I realize just how hungry I was.

We ate around a deal table in the kitchen. 'So you like your new home?' Dad said. 'It's over seventy years old, you know. Belonged to a mine-owner many years ago. He had it specially built for him . . . so the estate agent told me.'

'It must have cost the earth,' I said.

Mum shook her head. 'Not really. Houses are much cheaper down here . . . especially large ones like this. But even so, I must admit we've got a bargain . . . '

'And finding it empty was a godsend,' my father added. 'Meant I could have my two favourite women down here with me.'

He smiled fondly and I remembered what Robert had once said over breakfast about how concerned he'd been. I resolved there and then to accept the inevitable and make the best of what I was still convinced was going to be a bad job.

When we'd finished lunch, Mum suggested I should explore the garden. 'It goes right down to the river,' she said, placing a bowl of fresh fruit on the table. 'And it's very pretty . . . really it is . . . '

Picking up a juicy pear, I wandered into the garden.

The air was mild and gentle and with the glare of the September sun strong in my eyes, I ambled across the wide lawn to the apple tree. To my left was a vegetable garden, depleted now of vegetables, except for two rows of runner beans climbing drunkenly up long bamboo sticks. I followed a winding path made of crazy paving and went down five steep steps to another lawn. On the bank, aubretia and heathers still bloomed and as I walked across the springy turf I saw that the conifers did not mark the end of the garden. Beyond was a patch of waste ground, a riot of weeds and wild flowers which ended at the river.

And at the river, in our garden, was a boy.

I watched him for a moment. He was about my age with a thatch of straight dark hair with the merest suggestion of a wave. Dressed in jeans and a check shirt, he held a fishing-rod in his hands. Skilfully, he cast his line into the centre of the pool.

Then, as I was about to demand what he was doing, trespassing in our garden, he brought back his rod. The line snaked through the air, flicking droplets of water as it curved over his shoulder. Of course, I had to be standing in the wrong place at the wrong time. The hook sank into my sweater. Then he gave the line a jerk.

'Hey! Watch what you're doing!' I yelled as he tried to cast me, as well as his bait, into the water.

I have never seen a guy jump so violently.

Chapter 4

He spun round at the sound of my angry voice and gaped as though he'd never seen a girl in his life. Then, recovering, he hurried towards me.

'Hey. I'm sorry . . . I didn't see you standing behind me.' The soft Welsh lilt to his voice sounded like music in my ears. But it wasn't that which made me catch my breath – or the fact that he was taller than I'd first assumed. It was his eyes. They were dark brown with a depth and clarity that made me feel weak. And he had the longest eyelashes I'd ever seen on a guy.

'Hold on!' Deftly, he threaded the hook through my sweater and, taking a knife from his pocket, cut through the line. 'I don't think I've done any damage.'

He looked down at me, and the smile that came so naturally to his lips melted the anxious concern in his eyes, and once more I found myself catching my breath. Then he went and spoilt it.

'But what were you doing there anyway?' he said. 'It was a stupid thing to do. You should have known better than to stand right behind someone who was casting.'

'Oh was it?' His bluntness annoyed me and I began to think that first impressions could certainly be deceptive.

'Of course it was. The hook could have sunk right into you.'

The concern was there in those dark eyes again and once more I felt butterflies fluttering deep inside my stomach.

'You haven't answered me. What were you doing there?'

'I might well ask you the same question,' I said stiffly.

He shrugged his broad shoulders. 'I was fishing, wasn't I?'

'That was obvious. But you happen to be fishing from my garden.'

He looked at me in disbelief and then glanced up at the house. 'You're kidding. The house is empty . . . '

'Not any more it isn't!' My reply was defiant.

37

He glanced again at the house, where a curtain caught by the breeze was fluttering from an open window.

'Hey. You're right . . . someone is living there . . . '

'And that someone happens to be me.'

Suddenly, he was like a little boy caught out in some act of mischief. He ran a hand awkwardly through his hair. 'Looks as if I'm trespassing, doesn't it?'

He made me want to smile, but I wasn't going to let him off the hook so soon. And certainly not after the way he had hooked me.

'Yes you are.' I said loftily.

My attitude made him seem even more vulnerable. 'Your parents. Do you think they'll mind? I mean . . . I wouldn't have come here if I'd known . . . '

It took all my power to control the smile that was lurking around my lips.

'Perhaps I'd better go,' he went on, 'before they see me . . . '

I couldn't pretend any longer. A giggle burst from deep inside my throat and the frown on his tanned forehead disappeared as understanding dawned. 'You're having me on . . . ' Laughter and incredulity were mixed now. 'You don't live here at all . . . '

'Oh yes I do . . . ' I didn't try to hide my amusement. 'And I *am* teasing you . . . I'm sure my parents won't mind you being here . . . '

At that moment, I heard my mother calling me, and a second or two later, she appeared on the path.

'Oh, I'm sorry. I didn't know you had company . . . ' She smiled and picked her way through the long grass. 'Well, aren't you going to introduce your friend to me . . . ?'

It was my turn to be confused. I glanced at him. 'I'm

sorry . . . I don't know your name . . . '

He gave a small apprehensive cough. 'It's Gareth . . . Gareth Morgan.'

Mum nodded her head in acknowledgement. 'It's nice to meet you, Gareth . . . ' Then a puzzled frown grooved her forehead. 'But how did you get here? I didn't notice anyone come past the house . . . '

Gareth went red with embarrassment. 'I happened to be fishing . . . '

Hurriedly, I butted in. 'He was on the other side of the river. I told him he could fish from our side if he wanted to . . . '

He flashed me a look of gratitude. 'That's if you don't mind,' he said.

'Of course I don't mind. Why on earth should I?' Then she must have had a lightning second thought, because she added. 'Though I wouldn't tell too many people if I were you. I don't fancy being invaded by an army of anglers . . . '

She looked awkwardly at us both for a moment. 'I suppose I'd better get back to the house . . . and do some more unpacking . . . ' She walked back up the gentle slope until she reached the trees. 'I almost forgot. I came to tell you the coffee's ready. Why don't you ask Gareth if he'd like one too?'

I glanced shyly at him. 'Well, would you? Like a cup of coffee?'

He grinned at me. 'Yeah. Why not?'

'What about your fishing?'

'It doesn't really matter. I can do that any time. And anyway the fish are not biting this afternoon.' He followed me back to the house. 'By the way,' he said. 'I don't know your name yet.'

'It's Claire . . . Claire Courtney . . . '

He held out his hand. 'Nice to meet you, Claire. And thanks for covering up for me like that . . .'

'It was nothing. I could see you were embarrassed . . .'

He scratched his head. 'Yeah. I was, wasn't I? Funny! That's not like me at all . . .'

We reached the kitchen and Gareth, leaving his gear on the patio, followed me inside. Mum and Dad were already sitting round the table sipping their coffees.

'Hello, Gareth,' Dad stood up and held out his hand. He'd obviously been well briefed by my mother. 'I hear you're a keen angler. What do you catch?'

'People mostly,' I said, and told them what had happened.

They both laughed and Gareth grinned in that attractive selfconscious way I was beginning to know. Dad went on asking him questions about freshwater fishing, though I knew that he'd never been interested in angling in his life. I became embarrassed at the third-degree treatment Garet was enduring, and so did my mother, because she interrupted my father.

'Do let the boy drink his coffee, Derrick,' she scolded, and held out a plate of chocolate biscuits. 'Help yourself, Gareth.'

Then she thrust a biscuit into my father's open mouth. 'That's to keep you quiet,' she said.

Of course, Dad wasn't going to be put off by a simple admonition from my mother and within five minutes, he'd discovered that Gareth lived on a housing estate nearer town, that his father worked in a bank in Swansea, and that he was a sixth-form pupil at Pencarnog Comprehensive School.

'So is Claire,' he said. 'At least she will be next week.'

Gareth turned eagerly to me. 'Will you really?'

I nodded. 'Though I'm not looking forward to it . . . '

'Why not? It's not a bad school as schools go . . . some of the teachers are almost human . . . ' He pondered for a moment. 'Though I'm not sure I can say that about the headmaster . . . '

My father was about to ask him another question when my mother tapped him on his shoulder. 'Drink up your coffee, Derrick,' she ordered. 'We've got work to do.'

It was a blatant ploy on the part of my mother to get him to leave me and Gareth together, but it didn't work. Gareth jumped to his feet.

'Is there anything I can do to help, Mr Courtney?' he said. 'I haven't got anything important on this afternoon.'

My mother pursed her lips and gave a slight shake of the head. Dad, however, either didn't see her or chose to ignore her gesture. 'It's very good of you, Gareth. I certainly could do with an extra pair of hands. But are you sure it won't be taking you away from something else?'

'No, of course not, Mr Courtney. Like I told Claire earlier. The fish aren't biting today.'

It didn't take long for my father to come to a decision. 'All right, Gareth. If you're sure you don't mind, I'd be very grateful for your help.'

Gareth shot me a grin and followed Dad into the hall to carry some crates to the attic. When Mum and I were alone she smiled mischievously at me.

'Looks like you've made a conquest there, my girl,' she said.

My cheeks began to burn. 'Don't be ridiculous, Mum. I've only just met him . . . '

'That's what I mean. You've only just met him and already he's prepared to do anything to please your father. In my book, that can only mean one thing . . . '

Her words made a feeling of warmth run through my body that had nothing to do with the embarrassment I'd felt a few seconds earlier. Gareth was a nice looking guy and in the short time I'd known him, I found he was fun to be with.

But then I thought of Simon. And it was as though someone had thrown a bucket of iced water over me. How could I think of Gareth in that way, I scolded myself, when only twenty-four hours earlier Simon and I had vowed to be true to each other, declaring that nothing could possibly keep us apart for ever.

It was almost three hours later when Gareth left, after having had tea and cake with us and seemingly enjoying every minute he'd spent lugging heavy boxes around the house.

'See you in school on Monday then,' he said as I accompanied him to the door.

'Well . . . ' I began doubtfully. 'I'm not sure about Monday. Mum has planned to do some shopping in Swansea then . . . ' I gave a little grimace, ' . . . for my school uniform. Most probably it'll be Tuesday.'

Gareth shrugged his shoulders happily. 'Great. See you Tuesday instead.' He was half-way down the drive when he turned. 'Hey,' he yelled. 'Thought you'd like to know something. You're the biggest thing I've hooked this year . . . '

Then, with a laugh and a jaunty wave of the hand, he ran down the road.

When I returned to the kitchen, Mum was doing the washing-up. Dad nodded at the clock on the wall.

'Better get ready,' he said. 'The Evanses are expecting us at seven.'

Mum flicked him with the dishcloth. 'If that's the case, you'd better give me a hand with the washing-up instead of munching that last cake . . . '

He picked up a cloth, dried the dishes and stacked them away. I sat on a chair and watched him.

'Do I have to go, Dad?' I couldn't imagine anything worse than being incarcerated with some of Dad's friends. He and Mr Evans would probably talk business, while Mum and Mrs Evans would exchange recipes or knitting patterns or something equally revolting. I could see myself being stuck there trying to look interested and getting more and more uptight with every tick of the clock. 'I'd much rather stay here and watch television.'

My father frowned. 'You can't do that, Claire. They've especially asked you to come . . . '

'Why me?'

'Because they'd like you to meet their daughter.'

It was worse than I thought. She was probably a spotty little kid in the second form who'd sit there giggling all evening.

'Her name is Rhiannon and she's in the Sixth Form . . . like your friend Gareth . . . '

I leaned forward. 'What did you say her name was?'

He wiped his hands and leaned against the sink unit. 'It's a Welsh name,' he explained unnecessarily. 'And it's pronounced Ree – an – on. And she's nice. In fact, she's very pretty . . . '

'Oh, is she?' Mum pretended to be jealous. 'Trust you to notice.'

She threw the dishcloth at him. It hit him squarely in

the face and fell on to the clean white shirt he'd just changed into.

My father was not amused!

But he was right about Rhiannon. She really was pretty. As we found out when she opened the door to us. We had travelled back along the road into town, turned left at a small pub before entering a large modern housing estate. Mr Evans' house wasn't as large as ours though it was modern – with an integral garage and Georgian-style windows.

My father rang the bell and we heard the chimes sing a tune. A few seconds later the door opened and a girl roughly my own age stood there.

She was shorter than me, and had the most gorgeous red hair I had ever seen. It had been brushed up so that it was light and fluffy, and the sun slanting through a window in the hall made it appear a rich golden halo around her head. But though her skin was fair, her eyes were unusually dark.

'Please come in,' she said with a welcoming smile. 'My parents are in the lounge . . . '

She took our coats and opening a door, ushered us in. She smiled again when I hung back.

'Hello, Claire,' she said. 'My name's Rhiannon . . . but I expect you already know that . . . '

I took an instant liking to her, and knew without doubt that she would become one of my closest friends. In just a few hours, I had met two people who were to have a major influence on my life in Pencarnog – but not in quite the way I imagined.

Chapter 5

Dinner was a polite pleasant affair and Rhiannon's parents did everything to make us feel welcome. Towards the end of the meal, Mrs Evans turned to me.

'And what do you think of Wales so far?' she asked, passing me a cup of coffee.

About the same age as my mother, she had Rhiannon's red hair, though hers had dulled to a rich auburn.

It was a difficult question to answer. 'It's not like I thought it would be . . . it's strange to feel so enclosed . . . '

'Enclosed?'

My mother interrupted. 'I expect she means by the mountains . . . I know I felt the same when I first came down . . . come to think of it, I still do. You see, where we live . . . ' She hastily corrected herself. ' . . . where we lived was the highest point for miles . . . '

'It was called Hilltop Close,' interjected my father. 'Though if you saw the place, you'd probably laugh . . . it wasn't even a hill . . at least not as you know it . . . by the way,' he turned to Mr Evans. 'What's happened to all the coal-mines . . . I haven't seen one yet . . . '

Mr Evans laughed. 'And you won't either. The nearest one is over ten miles away . . . incidentally, did you know your house was built by one of the richest mine-owners in the district?' He went into an enthusiastic account of local history – obviously his hobby – and Rhiannon rolled her eyes at me.

It didn't go unnoticed, because Mrs Evans, suppressing a grin, said to Rhiannon.'Why don't you take Claire up to your room? You could play that record you bought this morning.' She didn't need to be asked twice.

'Come on, Claire,' she said. 'This way we might get out of the washing-up as well . . . '

I didn't argue. I just followed her to her room.

'Excuse the mess,' she said, picking up various items of underwear and a black school skirt which were lying on the floor. 'Mum's always nagging me about the way I keep my bedroom. Not that it does much good . . . ' She pulled a towel off the back of a green and gold basket chair, offered me a seat and flung herself down on her bed. 'You must excuse my father. Once he starts talking about local history, there's no stopping him.' She rolled over on to her side. 'Tell me. What's it like where you come from?'

Her question made me think of Simon and I told her of all the good times we'd had together. Rhiannon listened while I enthused about the tennis club we belonged to and the long walks we took along the bank of the river.

'And you left all that to come here?' she commiserated. 'To Pencarnog?'

'I didn't have much choice, did I? I had to. There was nothing else I could do.'

She shook her head in sympathy. 'I know. And to think you lived only fifty miles from London. I bet you went there every weekend . . . '

I shook my head. 'Not really. I don't think we went

there more than five or six times a year.'

'You didn't? Well, I would.' She leaned back on her pillow defiantly. 'I'd give anything to be where all the action is. I'll tell you something for nothing; when eventually I finish university and get myself a job, you won't get me within two hundred miles of this place . . . it's dead . . . it's like being buried alive.'

Her words did nothing to improve my morale. Then I thought of Gareth and the way he'd made me laugh that afternoon. 'But what about the fellas? Surely there must be some nice guys around.'

'Oh them! Don't talk to me about them! They're all right if you can get them away from their precious Rugby . . . Honestly, you might find this hard to believe, but it's like a religion around here. A girl doesn't stand a chance . . . '

Robert had laughingly warned me about that a few days before we left. 'That's what my brother said. It's Rugby first and girls second.'

Rhiannon levered herself up on one arm. 'Don't you believe it!' she replied hotly. 'It's Rugby first, second, third . . . we girls come way down in the pecking order . . . just slightly ahead of Saturday afternoon shopping.'

'Oh, it's like that, is it?'

'Worse. Honestly, trying to get them to come out with you before six o'clock on a Saturday is an absolute impossibility. It's school Rugby in the morning, and town Rugby in the afternoon . . . and if there are any action replays on the television in the evening, you can forget it . . . '

I thought of Gareth again. 'Not all, surely. There was one guy fishing at the bottom of our garden this afternoon . . . '

She pondered for a moment. 'That's because Pencarnog are playing away. He probably didn't have the money to follow them. And anyway what was he doing? Fishing. It's always something else. I tell you, they're impossible.' She looked at me again. 'Did you say you had a brother?'

'Yes . . . Robert.'

She sat up. 'That's interesting. How old?'

'Nineteen . . . going on twenty.'

She swung her legs off the bed. 'Really? Is he living with you?'

Her eagerness amused me. 'I'm afraid not. He's at university . . . Bristol.'

She slumped back on her bed. 'Trust. We could do with some new faces around here too . . . .'

'It wouldn't do any good,' I teased. 'He's mad about Rugby as well.'

She gave a loud groan. 'Fantastic. You can't win, can you?'

'But what do you do on weekends if the boys keep to themselves?' I asked, wondering what sort of world I'd entered.

'Saturday nights are usually all right. Girls are all right on Saturday nights . . . and Sundays if you're lucky . . . or any other night come to that if you haven't got much homework . . . ' She paused. 'Always assuming there isn't an evening match on, of course.'

'But where do you go on Saturday nights?' I asked, remembering that I hadn't seen any cinemas or dancehalls as we'd come through town.

'If it's a special occasion we go to Swansea . . . but normally we go to the Troubador.'

'The Troubador?'

'It's a dance-hall in the town centre right next to the shopping precinct.'

I frowned. 'I don't remember seeing it.'

'You probably wouldn't. It's behind the High Street. How would you fancy coming tonight? It'll give you the chance to meet the local talent . . . if you can call it that.'

I didn't think my mother would mind, though she'd probably say something ridiculous like I was too tired or something.

'All right,' I replied, after the briefest of pauses. 'I think I'd like that . . . '

'There's one thing though. It doesn't start swinging until about half-past ten . . . and closing time's one o'clock. Any problems?'

Knowing my parents, there were sure to be. I knew only too well how anxious they were whenever I was out late. But I just shook my head.

'I shouldn't think so,' I replied airily. 'I suppose I'll have to check it out with my parents first though . . . you know what they're like . . . '

Rhiannon nodded. 'Don't I just. Do you know! At one time, Dad used to insist on coming to get me. Would you believe it? Coming to pick me up as though I were a little kid!'

I knew what it was like. I'd been through it all myself. 'But he doesn't any more?' I said.

She shook her head with a grin. 'I reckon he got the message in the end . . . when I used to scowl. Anyway, when he saw there was always a crowd of us walking home together, he stopped coming to get me. Though I don't think he was very happy about being kept out of bed.'

As she spoke, I wondered if Dad would insist on

picking me up. It would be just my luck if he did. Then another, more important, thought struck me.

'What do you wear?' I said in alarm as I tried to think if I had anything suitable which didn't need ironing.

'You can suit yourself,' she replied. 'I normally wear jeans and a T-shirt.'

I gave a sigh of relief; jeans and T-shirts were my staple clothes.

So I decided to go downstairs and ask my parents if I could join Rhiannon at the disco. There was inevitably the moment's hesitation and the concerned glances when I told them the time I'd be coming home.

Surprisingly, it was Rhiannon's father who came to my rescue. 'She'll be quite safe,' he reassured them. 'I shall be giving them a lift down . . . ' He laughed when he saw the sudden flash of warning in Rhiannon's eyes. 'It's all right, miss. You can walk home with your friends if you like . . . ' He turned to my parents. 'There's a big crowd of them. I wouldn't fancy anyone's chances if they tried it on. Of course, if you think it's too late for Claire to be out . . . '

My mother shook her head. 'I'm sure neither of us minds her going,' she said. 'It was kind of Rhiannon to ask . . . '

The Troubador was part of the Town's new shopping centre, a large building made of brick and concrete that adjoined the cattle market, though it had a separate entrance on the side which faced the river. We walked hurriedly from the large car park where Mr Evans had dropped us, along an open covered-way, until we arrived at the double swing doors bathed in a shaft of light. A small crowd had gathered outside. Gradually, we shuffled out of the keen wind which had risen until we stood in the warmth of a rectangular entrance hall.

From an open doorway we could hear the rhythmic beat of one of the latest pop tunes.

Within a couple of minutes we had paid our entrance fees, deposited our coats and were standing in a long room, lit only by the light from a bar which occupied the length of one wall. From the disco placed on a low platform in a far corner, pulsating coloured lights made flickering patterns on the bodies of the dancers. Rhiannon searched the room, standing on the tips of her toes to look over the shoulders of the people in front.

'Come on!' she yelled, her voice almost inaudible against the hypnotic throb of the music. 'The others have managed to find a table . . . the other side of the room.'

Together, we pushed through the crowd that ringed the entrance and weaved our way along the edge of the dance-floor to a cluster of girls seated on plastic chairs around a circular table. There was, I noticed, a conspicuous absence of boys and Rhiannon, who had obviously had the same thought, assured me that they would be along later.

'There must be something on T.V.' she said and, rolling her eyes, added, 'Like I said; first things first.'

They were a friendly crowd. She introduced me to all five, though in the noise and excitement, I only remembered the name of one of them: Elin Pearce, a girl with long dark hair which tumbled over her shoulders. Soon I felt quite at home and as we sat there and they threw questions at me, they cooed with envy when they heard how close I lived to London. It was, I discovered, their

Mecca. And it was their unanimous decision that coming to live in Pencarnog was most certainly a retrograde step. And in spite of their friendliness and the easy way in which they had accepted me into their company, I just had to agree with them.

Then I felt a tap on my shoulder. I turned to find that the boys had arrived, led by no other than Gareth Morgan.

'Hey. Fancy seeing you here,' he said, his eyes shining with delight.

'I came with Rhiannon,' I explained, 'We had dinner with her parents and she asked me along.'

'Now, why didn't I think of that . . . I could have asked you this afternoon, couldn't I?'

Rhiannon, however, was surprised. 'I didn't know you two had already met,' she said.

'Don't you remember? I told you about him . . . the one who was fishing at the bottom of our garden . . . '

'Ah! So it was you, Gareth Morgan.' She said it as though it explained a lot of things. 'Trust you to land yourself in trouble.'

Gareth grinned and shook his head. 'But I didn't land myself in trouble, did I? I helped Claire's father carry crates into the attic. And her mother asked me to stay for tea . . . '

'That's even worse.' She winked at me. 'That makes you the biggest creep in Pencarnog . . . '

Gareth held up his hands in defeat. 'All right. All right. I give in. You win. Now, if I promise to buy you both another lager . . . will you promise not to tell anyone else?'

I wasn't sure whether or not I should have another one. I didn't want my father smelling drink on my breath and perhaps stopping me meeting them again.

'Make it your last one then,' said Gareth, taking the empty glass from my hand and going to the bar.

'Fancy you meeting him of all people,' Rhiannon said in disbelief. 'Gareth Morgan . . . Captain of the School Rugby Team and the biggest male chauvinist in the area . . .'

I didn't know whether to believe her or not. It didn't sound like the fella I'd met in the garden that afternoon.

Chapter 6

I found it difficult to get to sleep that night. I lay in my bed listening to the chuckling sound of the river as it gurgled over rounded pebbles; in the distance a fox barked, a strange eerie sound that made me shiver. There was no moon and the window was a faint glimmer against a sky punctured by myriad stars; since there were no street lamps at the rear of the house, the darkness was so intense, it lay like a suffocating blanket over the whole room.

I shut my eyes tightly and thought of Simon, though once again I had to concentrate really hard to conjure up his face. It was a strange feeling. I felt as though I were isolated – shipwrecked in a kind of limbo between two worlds; England which lay behind me and Wales which I had yet to meet and know properly. I felt so unreal, and it was only the memory of Simon now strong in my mind that gave me any sense of belonging.

Eventually, whether it was the sheer effort of keeping my eyes tightly shut or the soporific murmur of the river, I fell into a slumber so deep that I didn't even dream.

It was almost eleven the next morning before I awoke; a hand, shaking me gently on my shoulder, brought me blinking into the world again.

'My goodness. You really were asleep, weren't you?' Mum handed me a steaming mug of coffee and sat on the edge of the bed. 'Not surprising, considering the time you arrived home last night. Lucky for you your father was in such a good mood.'

I sat up and yawned, remembering the previous evening. When we'd left the disco, we all walked to the fork in the road where we had to part company; Rhiannon, Elin, Gareth and the others to the right and up a gentle rise to a small plateau on the side of the hill; while I alone had to walk the two or three hundred yards up the Carmarthen road. That road was dark, particularly where some large trees overhung the pavement, enveloping the street lights and casting deep gloomy shadows over the ground. Sensing my uneasiness, they all decided to accompany me to my door.

My mother smiled gently at me. 'And did you enjoy yourself?'

'Oh, yes!' I nodded. 'I met so many people . . . most of them in the Sixth Form . . . they were great . . . '

'I am glad. And now . . . ' She pushed herself off the bed. 'I suppose I'd better get the house into some kind of order. And you, miss, can give me a hand.'

Half an hour later, when I'd emerged from the bathroom, I went downstairs and helped myself to bowlful of cereal. My father was already unpacking a tea-chest containing crockery, handing it carefully to my mother who was washing it.

'What can I do?' I asked.

'How about getting yourself a tea-towel,' my mother suggested. 'Then you can put these things in the cupboard. Cups and saucers to the right . . . plates to the left.' She indicated the wall cabinets above her head. 'All other things down below . . . '

We worked really hard for the next hour so that it was almost one o'clock by the time we were able to sit down to a lunch of cold chicken and salad.

Then, over coffee, my father announced to my relief that work was over for the day and that he was going to sit in front of the television set in the living-room and allow it to lull him to sleep. My mother decided that it was a good idea and said she would join him. Which left me on my own.

The sun by this time had moved round to the rear of the house, so, armed with a glass of fresh orange juice, I ambled on to the patio and sat under the shade of a large umbrella which my father had salvaged from the garage. It was so peaceful, the air so balmy, that I began to feel at ease with the world. I thought fondly of Simon and longed to hear his voice again.

And then, as though in response to my wishes, the phone rang. It's him, I thought; it must be. I jumped to my feet and rushed into the house. Mum had got there before me and was cradling the receiver in her hand.

'It's him,' she whispered. 'Your boyfriend . . . Gareth . . . '

My heart sank. With an air of despondency I took the phone from her.

Gareth sounded nervous. 'I hope you don't mind me phoning. But I wondered if you'd like to come out . . . '

'What? Now?' The words came out far harsher than I'd intended.

'Yes . . . if you're not doing anything else, that is . . . I thought you might want to go for a walk . . . I could show you the town . . . '

I was about to refuse when I thought of his kindness the previous day. And I really wasn't doing anything at that moment.

'Of course if you've got something more important to do . . . ' he went on when I didn't reply.

'No . . . that will be great!' I replied, realizing how ill-mannered it would be to refuse. 'I'd like to see Pencarnog . . . very much . . . '

'Great.' His obvious pleasure made me smile to myself in spite of the fact that only minutes earlier I'd been feeling slightly moody over Simon. 'I'll pick you up in about ten minutes . . . if that's all right . . . '

He arrived long before I was ready. I was in my bedroom putting on some perfume when the doorbell rang and I heard my mother ask him in. A few minutes later, I ran lightly down the stairs to find him in the living-room talking to my father. The look of approval he gave as I walked in made me feel warm all over.

'Gareth's taking me round Pencarnog,' I explained, slightly breathlessly. 'I don't suppose we'll be long. . . '

We walked down the drive and turned left at the gate. 'Hey. Hold on. I thought you said you were going to show me the town . . . '

'So I am.'

'Then why are we walking away from it?'

He grinned at me. 'I said I'd show you Pencarnog . . . I didn't say I'd walk you round it.' He pointed to the hill on the opposite side of the road. 'We're going up there, where we can see much better.'

'Oh!' I said, suddenly understanding. 'A kind of bird's-eye view!'

'Something like that,' he answered with a nod.

We crossed the road and eventually came to a track that led to a farm. I held back as he opened a sagging metal gate.

'Are you sure it's all right? Won't the farmer mind?'

'Oh course he won't. As long as you don't leave the gates open behind you . . . or frighten the bulls . . .'

'Bulls!' I'd never been close to cattle before and the prospect frightened me.

'They're all right as long as you don't wave a red flag at them.'

Now I knew he was kidding. 'Oh, stop it, Gareth!' I chided. 'You had me worried for a moment.'

We went through two more sets of gates, crossed a cobbled farmyard in front of a squat whitewashed farmhouse and entered a sunken lane that led up the hill. Presently, we came to another gate which marked the limit of the farmer's land. Beyond was bare mountainside covered with bracken. We thrust our way through, following a narrow winding path which led steadily upwards. At last, it levelled off and we came to a flat shelf about a hundred yards long, cut into the hillside, revealing a sheer rock face with broken boulders at its base.

'It's the remains of an old quarry,' Gareth explained as I looked up at its sheer ruggedness. 'You'll find several around here.'

'But what were they digging for?'

'Stone, of course! It's what the town is built of. They quarried it, carted it down the hill and used it to build houses.' He searched in the long grass and turned over a small boulder; the underside was fresh and clean.

'See? It's the same colour as your house. But that's not what I brought you up here for . . .' He walked to the edge and beckoned me to follow. 'Come and have a look at this.'

I stood on the brink of the quarry and gazed with bated breath at the panorama in front of me. Until that moment, I hadn't realized how high we'd climbed, or even how far we'd come from our house. It was way below to my right, a small doll's house set in a miniature garden with a river at the end that looked more like a brook as it gleamed in the strong sunlight.

'Now you can see Pencarnog properly,' he said.

Two main roads formed a cross in the centre of the town, while the river curved in an arc to the south, meandering to the sea about twenty or more miles away.

Gareth put his arm on my shoulder. 'That's the road to Carmarthen,' he pointed to the road which led past our house. 'And that one . . . ' I followed the direction of his finger, ' . . . that one leads to Swansea. The motorway's just behind the hill.'

It was like looking down at a living map. Cars no bigger than beetles crawled along the intersecting roads, coming to a halt at the traffic lights before continuing on their journey, and the few people who were about really did look like ants.

'And now come and have a look at this.'

He led me further along until we were looking down at the older part of town, its streets straight and regular.

'There it is.' He pointed proudly at an emerald green field, set in the centre of the older houses, and about four hundred yards from the town centre itself. 'That's the Rugby field.'

I remembered what both Robert and Rhiannon had said about rugby being a kind of religion in Wales and I smiled mischievously to myself as an idea struck me.

'Oh, yes.' I pretended to be unimpressed. 'So what? Rugby's a stupid old game, anyway.'

I felt his arm stiffen around my shoulder. Then he turned slowly, a look of absolute horror on his face.

'Rugby? A stupid game?'

'Of course. Thirty men chasing a deformed ball . . .'

He shook his head, appalled at my words. 'Do you know what you're saying? You can't possibly mean it . . .'

His shock was so genuine and the reaction to my words so comical that I just burst out laughing.

'Oh, Gareth . . .' Tears came to my eyes and I had to shake my head to blink them away. 'You and your Rugby!'

Slowly, it sank in that I'd been teasing and he gave a sigh of relief. 'Claire!' he said. 'Don't ever do that again. Not to me or anyone else. Others might not be quite as forgiving as I am . . .'

We were walking back home when he suddenly turned to me. 'Hey. You didn't tell me your father was the new manager at the electronics factory.'

'You didn't ask,' I replied, trying to keep my balance as we returned through the bracken.

'True.' he conceded. 'It didn't half surprise me though when Rhiannon told me last night. I mean. . . . I'd been helping one of the most important men in Pencarnog . . .'

'Important? I'm sure my father doesn't think of himself like that.

'Perhaps not.' He paused as he opened the farm gate. 'But that's what he is. Look at it like this, Claire. Your father's factory is the biggest one for miles around . . . Pencarnog depends on it for jobs . . . which makes your father exactly what he is. Important.'

I hadn't thought of it like that before, and though it made me feel proud, I understood too what a terrible responsibility it placed upon him. I knew from what he'd told my mother that the factory hadn't been as successful as it should have been, which was why he'd been sent to take over.

But what if he failed? I thought. He wouldn't be the only one to lose his job. Many others in Pencarnog would too.

Gareth nudged my shoulder. 'You haven't been listening to a word I've been saying, have you?'

I blinked in surprise. 'I'm sorry . . . I was thinking . . .'

'I know . . . I asked if you'd like to come to watch Pencarnog playing next Saturday.'

I had the feeling it was the highest compliment he could pay a girl; to ask her to a rugby match.

I smiled and nodded. 'All right. I think I'd like that very much.'

Gareth wouldn't come in to tea, and later as I helped my mother butter the bread I told her what Gareth had said about Dad's importance to the community.

'I'm sure he's right,' she said, placing a sponge cake in the centre of the table. 'But I'm equally sure there's nothing to worry about either. Your father only mentioned this afternoon that the situation at work is far better than he expected it to be.'

I didn't know whether to believe her or not. There was something in her attitude that made me suspicious, but before I could question her further, she said something that made me really angry.

'Oh, by the way. Simon phoned when you were out. He asked if you could ring him back before half past four.'

I gave a cry of exasperation, looked at the clock, and discovered it was a quarter to five.

'Oh, Mum. Why didn't you tell me earlier?'

'I'm sorry, darling. I forgot.'

But I wasn't listening. I was dashing to the hall to dial Simon's number.

It was his mother who answered. 'Oh, Claire, it's you . . . I'm sorry, but Simon's just left . . . with some of his friends.'

I felt my heart sink to the bottom of my stomach. 'Do you happen to know when he'll be back?' I asked.

Of course she didn't, though she promised to tell him I phoned. We spoke for a couple of minutes and then rang off.

I returned to the tea table and sat there morosely, wishing that my mother could have told me earlier about Simon's phone call. Why, oh why did she have to forget when she knew how important it was to me?

And then, as I gazed bleakly at my father, a horrible feeling came over me, making me feel so cold that my flesh began to creep. I couldn't explain why. Perhaps it might have been because of my disappointment at not having been able to speak to Simon. Or it might have been as a result of what Gareth had said.

But suddenly I knew that trouble lay ahead. Serious trouble that would affect us all. Me more than anyone else.

Chapter 7

The visit to Swansea which my mother had planned
did not take place after all. Rhiannon's mother had
phoned to tell her that one of the outfitters in Pencarnog stocked the official school uniform, which, it
turned out, consisted only of a black skirt, white
blouse, grey pullover and a green and black striped tie.

'So we won't go, if you don't mind,' my mother said
over breakfast. 'Another time perhaps . . . when we've
settled in . . .'

I didn't mind. Overnight thick cloud had drifted in
from the west, enveloping the hills and bringing down
a clammy grey mist which hung like a shroud over
everything. As I stared miserably out of the window,
the apple trees a faint shape in the drizzling rain, I felt
cold in spite of the fact that Mum had switched on the
central heating.

We spent the day working in the bedrooms, unpacking the assortment of boxes which hadn't been
taken to the attic, and it was past three o'clock before
Mum was able to drive us into town.

By now, a keen wind was whipping down from the
hills, driving the rain before it, and in the few minutes it
took to hurry to the shops, my legs were soaked and
my hair was plastered to my head.

If this is Wales, I thought, you can keep it.

The only good thing that happened that day was Simon's phone call. It came just as I came out of the bath and, clutching the huge robe around me, I took the phone from my mother and huddled on the bottom stair.

'Sorry I was out when you phoned,' he said, 'I went out with some of my mates to this pop concert in Reading.'

'Lucky you,' I responded gloomily. 'They don't seem to have things like that down here.'

He went on to tell me what it had been like, how much they had enjoyed themselves and how they'd arrived home at three o'clock in the morning.

'Wish you'd been there with me though,' he added.

Up till that moment, his words had depressed me. Now I brightened up. 'Do you really?'

'Of course. You know how much I miss you, Claire.'

I sat there, perched on the bottom stair, talking to him happily for the next few minutes, until he said he had to ring off.

'Dad had a hefty phone bill this quarter,' he explained. 'I have to go easy. I'll phone you again next week.'

For the rest of the evening, I felt happy and sad at the same time and when I arose next morning, I still felt the same.

'Now are you sure you don't want me to come with you?'

We were just finishing our breakfast and Mum as usual was treating me as though I were a little kid.

'Oh, Mum. Of course I am. I'm quite capable of going to school on my own. You'll be wanting to hold my hand next . . .'

She smiled indulgently. 'I realize that. But since it's a

new school and you have to see the deputy headmaster before you can be admitted, I thought you might like to have me there. After all, when I phoned, he did say I could attend if I wanted to . . . '

I rolled my eyes in despair. 'But I can see him on my own. All he'll do is take my name and address and show me to my class.'

'All right. Don't get so excited. It was only a suggestion.' She glanced at the clock. 'You'd better get ready. You don't want to be late on your first day.'

The way I felt at that moment, I didn't care if I was late every day. Already my stomach felt as though tiny fingers were pulling it in all directions, making me feel sick and empty.

'It won't really matter, Mum. He won't be able to see me until after assembly. . . . and if I do go early, I'll have to hang outside his room for hours . . .'

She looked at me dubiously. 'Well . . . if you say so . . .' She thought for a moment, and then, remembering that I would have missed the school bus, insisted on running me into town. 'It's the least I can do, so let's not have any more arguments, shall we?'

'All right, Mum!' I replied wearily, knowing from experience that when my mother had made up her mind, nothing was going to change it. 'But only to the gate. I don't want you walking across the yard with me.'

Half an hour later she dropped me at the main gate. 'Good luck,' she called, leaning over the front seat and throwing me a kiss. 'See you tonight . . .'

I turned away quickly – just in case she threw me another kiss. Really! Mothers were quite impossible. Especially mine!

The school stood back about twenty yards from the

road and was built of the familiar local stone, though the low wall that ran alongside the pavement was of dark red brick. There were two entrances, one at each end, so I made for the nearest one. I found Elin standing just inside, armed with a dark green notebook. With her was another girl, short, with mousey-coloured hair.

'Claire!' Her welcome was warm and genuine. 'I wondered when you'd be starting . . . ' She turned to the other girl. 'This is Claire Courtney . . . you remember . . . I told you about her yesterday.' Then she introduced us. 'This is Jane, Jane Watkins . . . she's one of our gang but she couldn't make the Troubador last Saturday.'

She beamed a smile at me. 'So you're the one who lives in that big house on the Carmarthen road. Some people have all the luck . . . '

'And I have the strong feeling,' added Elin mischievously, 'that Gareth Morgan's taken a fancy to her . . . '

'Not *the* Gareth Morgan?'

'None other.'

Jane gave a deep chuckle. 'Better not let Rhiannon Evans find out then . . . or there's sure to be trouble. . .'

Their banter was making me go red. 'I've been told to report to the deputy headmaster,' I said quickly to hide my embarrassment. 'Any idea where I can find him?'

Elin glanced at her watch. 'He's in assembly at the moment. If you can wait a few minutes though I'll take you to his office . . . as soon as we've finished with this odious latecomer duty . . . '

Soon we heard the sound of voices from the rear of

the building and clusters of boys and girls began to cross the yard.

'Assembly's over.' Elin sighed with relief. 'Thank goodness this stupid duty's over for today. As if anyone bothers to come in through this entrance after nine. They've probably jumped over the wall at the back. Come on! I'll show you where Mr Mortimer's room is.'

I followed her to an entrance at the rear of the building, tucked at the side of the school hall, a new brick-built structure which dominated the quadrangle. She led me down a corridor, congested with pupils of all ages, until we came to his study, strategically placed on the ground floor at a point where two other corridors converged.

'I can't tell you how long he'll be,' Elin apologized. 'And I'm afraid I can't wait with you, but he should be along. Anyway, I'd better get to my class. See you later.'

She disappeared along the corridor, leaving me to run the gauntlet of curious and hostile stares from the mass of anonymous kids who passed by. Gradually the turmoil subsided and I was left alone with a scruffy boy dressed in jeans and a crumpled check shirt. The piece of string he wore round a buttonless collar was an apology for a tie. He looked at me once, glancing up and down as though I were something that had been dragged out of the gutter, and then studiously ignored me.

Presently, I heard footsteps marching down the corridor and a teacher appeared, his black gown streaming behind him as he swept round the corner. Dressed in a dark blue suit, he had thin hair streaked with grey and a large moustache that drooped from his upper lip. He flung open the door and barged into his room.

'Come in, Turner!' he ordered over his shoulder. 'And shut the door behind you.'

Turner levered himself off the wall and sauntered in with his hands in his pockets. Contempt oozed from every laconic movement.

'I said shut that door.' Mr Mortimer's command bounced off the walls and boomed along the corridor. 'And take your hands out of your pockets, you horrible boy . . .'

For about ten minutes, I heard him harangue Turner, warning him, and threatening him with all kinds of punishment if he didn't mend his ways. Eventually, the door opened and Turner emerged, looking as if the experience hadn't affected him in the slightest. He glanced at me, smirked with disdain, and swaggered along the corridor.

Then Mr Mortimer came out. 'Yes? Were you waiting to see me?'

His tone was now quite different and when I told him who I was, he actually beamed with approval. 'Of course. Claire Courtney. I spoke to your mother yesterday, didn't I?' It was hard to believe that only seconds before he had been bellowing at another pupil. 'Come in, Claire. Sit down. I'll just take some details . . .'

He went through the ritual of entering my name in a large black book, asked the name of my previous school, my 'O' level results, before inquiring about the subjects I wished to study in the Sixth Form.

'English, History and Art,' I told him.

He leaned forward, elbows on the table, fingers pressed together, nodding and smiling. The light shone on his bald head.

'Good. Good. And what about sports?'

'I played in the first hockey team at Priory Grange,' I replied.

'That's excellent.' The nodding went on. 'That should please Miss Reynolds. She's the head of our P.E. Department . . . always looking for good hockey players.' Then he sat back in his swivel chair and twirled gently from side to side. 'Well, I'm sure you'll be very happy with us . . . we all get on well together . . .'

He stood up abruptly. 'Now I'd better take you to the Sixth Form Block and introduce you to some of your teachers.' He picked up a loose-leaved file, flicked over some pages and consulted a timetable. 'Ah. The first year Sixth have English at this moment . . . let's go and see Mr Price, shall we?'

He led the way across the yard to a large modern two-storeyed building which stood apart from the rest of the school.

He opened the door which led into a small foyer. 'That's your common room,' he nodded to the right. Through the glass door, I saw several students lounging around on black vinyl armchairs. One or two were playing cards which they hastily concealed when they saw Mr Mortimer glaring in at them. But before I could have a closer look, he bounded up the flight of stairs and stopped outside a classroom.

He rapped briefly on the door and burst in. 'Ah. Mr Price. I have a new pupil for you. Claire Courtney. Come here from England, would you believe.'

Mr Price shook his head gravely. 'Then all I can say is, she must be mad.' He was in his mid-thirties, dark-haired and bearded. But as he spoke there was a twinkle in his eyes. 'Who in her right mind would deliberately want to associate with a shower like this. . . ' He waved his hand at a class of about twenty students seated around tables, among them Elin and Jane Watkins. There was a good-natured growl of disapproval.

'Silence, slaves,' he commanded. Then he grinned at me. 'You mustn't be too dismayed, Claire. They can be quite human at times . . . '

His insulting words, affectionately meant, brought another amiable response from his class. I knew immediately that Mr Price was going to be fun – so different to my previous English teacher, Miss Simpson, who had lacked even the slightest trace of humour.

At his suggestion, I joined Elin at her table. Meanwhile he and Mr Mortimer began to converse in a torrent of Welsh – my first introduction to the language.

It was my first introduction also to the infuriating habit I was to experience later when people spoke Welsh in front of me, not only leaving me effectively out of their conversation, but making me wonder what they were saying about me.

After the deputy head had left, Mr Price gave me some exercise books, a copy of the syllabus they were pursuing, a reading list, and enough set books to keep me busy for the rest of the year.

'You've missed almost three weeks' work, and as the others will tell you, that's a fair amount of work . . . '

There came the inevitable groan of agreement.

'So I'm afraid,' he continued 'that you're going to have a fair amount of catching up to do. Elin . . .' He began to speak to her in Welsh, then stopped. 'I'm sorry, Claire. I shouldn't have done that. It's a habit I must stop. I was just asking Elin if she'd let you borrow her books, that's all.'

We spent the rest of the lesson discussing *Pride and Prejudice*, which pleased me because Jane Austen was one of my favourite authors. Mr Price was pleasantly surprised when I contributed to the discussion and commented on it. Though as he did so, I had the distinct feeling that one or two of the class resented the newcomer who appeared to know so much. I made a mental note not to be quite so precocious in future. It wasn't, I realized, the best way to make friends.

Break was at ten-thirty. When the buzzer went, Mr Price dismissed us and I went to the common room with Elin where she introduced me to some of the girls who were pouring boiling water into rows of coffee mugs.

'We put twenty-five pence a week into the coffee swindle,' she explained as she handed me a mug. 'Rhiannon's in charge. You pay her every Monday. And talk of the devil, here she is.'

At that moment Rhiannon appeared at the door, her arms piled high with books. When she saw me, she hurried over, greeting me with her infectious smile.

'I heard you'd arrived,' she said breathlessly, dropping the books unceremoniously on to a chair. 'What do you think of the dump so far?'

It was the first time that morning that anyone had asked me that question and when I thought about it, I realized with a start that I liked it. I liked the warmth and welcome that everyone had extended to me. I liked Mr Mortimer, and I knew instinctively that Mr Price was going to be a great teacher.

'Yeah. They're not bad.' agreed Rhiannon. 'You'll find most of the others easy to get on with too.'

As I took a sip of my coffee, I glanced up to find that Gareth had just arrived, his head jewelled in minute droplets of rain. He grinned and waved across a crowded common room, and as he pushed a path towards me, I felt a flutter of sheer pleasure deep inside me.

Despite the incessant rain and the mist that made it necessary to have the lights on in the middle of the day, I had the sudden conviction that things were going to get better. Much better.

If only I could have foreseen the future.

Chapter 8

The rest of that week saw me settling in at school, getting to know more of the girls, especially Elin, who was turning out to be a very close friend. And of course, catching up with all the notes that Mr Price and all the other teachers had given during those first few weeks of term when I hadn't been anywhere near Pencarnog. I hardly had time to breathe.

Simon phoned on the Thursday evening and told me excitedly that he'd been invited to attend the selection centre at Biggin Hill for a medical examination and to sit some intelligence and aptitude tests.

'Isn't it great?' he said.

'Yes . . .of course . . .' I tried hard to sound enthusiastic but all I could think of was that in a few months he too would have left home and another of my links with the past would have been broken. 'When do you go?'

'Not for another month.' If my lack of enthusiasm had shown, he gave no sign that he'd noticed. 'I shall be staying there for about four days, and with a bit of luck they might let me know whether I'm accepted or not. . . .'

I felt sure he would be. 'Which means you'll be joining up in March, I suppose.'

'Yes . . . some time around then. Fantastic, isn't it?'

He went on talking about himself for about another five minutes, and then said, 'I've got to ring off now. Sorry . . . Dad wants to use the phone.'

Before I could say anything, the phone went dead, and I realized with a horrible sinking feeling in my stomach that this time he hadn't said he missed me. I felt suddenly isolated and found it almost impossible to settle down to my homework.

Even Mum noticed. She brought a cup of coffee to my room and sat on the edge of my bed.

'Look, Claire,' she said sympathetically. 'You really mustn't get so upset. You can't go on hankering for the past. You've got the present and the future to think of . . .'

'But Mum!' I was close to tears. 'I didn't want to live here, did I? I just had to . . .'

'So did I . . . I had to give up a lot . . . just as you did. But now that I am here, I'm determined to make the best of it.' She stood and squeezed my shoulder gently. 'Look on the bright side, darling. You've already made some very nice friends . . . that should make you happy at least.'

She was right, of course, and after she'd left, I forced

myself to think of Rhiannon and Elin – and Gareth – and strangely it seemed to work. It made me feel much much happier.

The next day was Friday and our one and only games lesson of the week. It was my first chance also to meet Miss Reynolds, the head of the P.E. Department who was, I discovered, not only the school hockey coach but had played for Wales in international matches. A fact all the girls seemed very proud of.

She bounced into the changing-room, her fair curly hair cut short. She clapped her hands together sharply.

'Quiet, girls . . . listen . . .' She waited until the chatter had subsided. 'We're not going to take long over our warming up exercises today . . . I'm still looking for players for our first team. So I'm going to split you into teams right now . . . that way we won't waste time on the field.' For the first time, she noticed me. 'I see we have a new girl.'

I told her my name and where I'd come from.

'You didn't happen to play hockey there by any chance?'

'Yes, Miss. I was in the first team last year.'

She was obviously impressed. 'Really? What position?'

'Right inner, Miss.'

'That's excellent. We could do with someone to back up Rhiannon and Elin . . . '

They were both sitting on the opposite side of the narrow room and when I glanced over, they smiled encouragingly. Miss Reynolds hurriedly organized us into teams, putting me into the same one as Rhiannon and Elin, and then clapped her hands sharply again.

'If everyone is ready, we'll make our way to the playing fields. And keep your voices down,' she ordered. 'Do remember, the rest of the school are still in classes.'

We trooped out of the gymnasium, walked around the side of the school and crossed the pedestrain bridge to the playing fields. Rhiannon dribbled a ball across the grass, pursued by Elin and me, and for a few minutes we had some informal passing practice.

Miss Reynolds blew her whistle and gathered us round her.

'Right. Four lengths of the pitch.' She ordered. 'Then back here for stretching exercises . . .'

There was a general groan and I was to discover that she was renowned for those exercises which went on far longer than I'd expected. We all gave a cheer when she announced that the game could begin.

Elin, Rhiannon and I played well together, almost as though we were on the same wavelength, and with Jane Watkins, at centre half, feeding the ball forward, we were a formidable team. The game was fast and since we were the stronger side, we had a far greater share of the ball.

Even Miss Reynolds remarked on it when we returned breathless to the school. 'I think I'll have to split you four up in future,' she said. 'It may well be good practice to play together, but it doesn't stretch you, does it? It doesn't prepare you for the opposition you'll get when you meet other schools.'

Then, as we clattered into the changing rooms, she took me aside. 'By the way, Claire, I was impressed by the way you played this afternoon. What would you say if I asked you to turn out for the first side a week tomorrow?'

What could I say? I just nodded enthusiastically,

feeling as though I was floating on a cloud and pleased by the way I was fitting into life at my new school.

That night, I decided to phone Dawn. Up until then I didn't know if I could have coped with hearing all the news of home without becoming depressed, but the events of that day had made me feel much more confident.

And talking to her would have been very pleasant if she had let me do just that. But all she wanted was to tell me about her and Julian.

'What about Simon?' I had managed to get a word in edgeways. 'Have you see him recently?'

'Well . . . ' she began. 'Yes and no . . . '

'Oh, Dawn, really! What do you mean "yes and no"?' 'Either you've seen him or you haven't.'

'That's just it,' she persisted. 'I have seen him . . . but only from a distance . . . '

Oh, great! I thought. You're a fine one for information.

I shouldn't have done that, because it gave her the chance to change the subject and go back to her and Julian again . . . about how she was missing him now that he was working in Chelmsford. She wasn't thinking about me at all. All I could do was sit there at the bottom of the stairs and seethe with frustration.

So when the front doorbell rang, I was glad of the excuse to put the receiver down. And even more glad to discover Gareth standing just inside the porch. He was dressed in smart blue jeans, a white sweatshirt and a light blue casual jacket. My heart gave a leap when I saw him.

'Hi!' He grinned down at me. 'Thought I'd come and make some arrangements for tomorrow.'

I stood aside to let him in.

'Tomorrow?' My brow furrowed as I tried to remember what was special about Saturday. 'What about tomorrow?'

'The Rugby match . . . Pencarnog are playing at home. You promised to come and watch them . . . remember?'

'Oh yes. Of course.' He followed me into the kitchen where I filled a kettle. 'Do you know. I'd forgotten . . . .I've had so much work to do . . . it's going to take me weeks to finish.'

'Anything I can do to help?'

I shook my head. 'Not really. It's just a lot of catching up on notes I've got to do . . . dead boring . . . '

'Do you fancy a coffee?' I asked.

'I don't mind. But actually I called to ask you round to my place tonight. I've asked Steve and Elin as well.'

'Who's Steve?'

'You haven't met him yet . . . he's been on a field study course for over a week.' Gareth leaned against the table and rubbed the side of his nose with a knuckle. 'He and Elin . . . they're going steady . . . '

I turned round in surprise. She hadn't told me she had a boyfriend; she hadn't even mentioned his name.

'Well, what do you say? Do you fancy coming?'

I returned the mugs I'd just taken from the cupboard. 'Just you try and stop me,' I replied. 'I want to know what this mysterious Steve looks like. He must be really something if Elin's too scared to tell anyone about him . . . '

We met him – and Elin – as we were trudging up the hill to Gareth's house. Tall and angular, with fair wavy hair that tumbled over his forehead he towered over

Elin as he walked beside her.

'Nice to meet you,' he said when Gareth introduced us. 'Do you know? This guy . . . ' He prodded Gareth in the ribs. 'This guy hasn't stopped talking about you . . . '

A low growl came from Gareth's throat. 'Cut it out, Bowen. You're asking for a thump . . . '

The threat did nothing to deter Steve. His grin became pronounced. 'Honestly, I couldn't wait to see the girl who's had so much effect on him . . . '

I hated to see Gareth so obviously embarrassed so I put my arm through his and squeezed it.

'And I couldn't wait to see the guy who's had so much effect on Elin,' I countered.

Elin's eyes opened wide in protest. 'Hey. Why bring me into it? What have I done?'

'Kept Steven a secret from us all,' I replied airily. 'That's what!'

'It's quite understandable really.' Gareth looked at me and winked. 'I mean . . . who in her right mind would want people to know she was going out with the ugliest guy in Pencarnog?'

Elin and Steven gave a simultaneous howl and began chasing us up the road.

We had a fantastic evening at Gareth's. His was a small semi-detached house, squeezed into a corner of a cul-de-sac, and overlooking the town. The lounge was only slightly larger than our kitchen, and it made me feel guilty to know that he, his brother and his two sisters had to share it. But the welcome his parents gave us dispelled my diffidence, so that soon I ignored the size of the room and enjoyed myself.

We talked and laughed and played records and shortly after nine o'clock, his mother came in with four steaming bowls of Welsh broth and a plateful of thickly cut fresh bread. It was the first time I'd tasted soup like it; rich with the taste of meat and a variety of vegetables, particularly leeks, it was one of the most delicious I'd ever eaten.

Later, Gareth walked me home. There was a full moon as we walked hand in hand down the hill. Below, the tops of the trees were bathed in its light, and the small patchwork fields were a pale misty green. I felt as though I were in a different world; a world where anything could happen.

All too soon, we reached our house and as we stood in the darkness of the porch, he asked me if I'd like to go to Swansea with him the following evening.

'My mother and father are going to see a film,' he explained. 'And they wondered if you'd like to come.'

I smiled mischievously to myself. 'Are they asking me? Or are you?'

'I . . . ' He stopped and looked at me suspiciously. 'I am, of course.'

'Ask me then. Idiot!'

'All right!' He put on a very formal voice. 'Would you like to come to Swansea with me tomorrow night?' Then he gave a deep-throated chuckle. 'If my mother lets . . . '

'Oh, you. Gareth Morgan!' I lifted my fist playfully, pretending to strike him. He grabbed it and for a moment looked down at me, grinning. The smile faded and, leaning closer, he kissed me . . . kissed me so gently that every nerve in my body tingled.

'See you tomorrow,' he whispered.

He called just after two and together we walked into town and joined the spectators who were streaming to the football stadium. As we got nearer, the crowd was funnelled into a narrow street and I had to stay close to him in case we became separated. Eventually, we squeezed through the turnstile and, making our way to the western end, stood on a small embankment which had once carried the railway line to Swansea.

'This is the best place . . . ' Gareth thrust his hands deeply into the pockets of his duffel coat. A wind had risen, a cold wind that seemed to whip down from the distant hills, and gust along the valleys. 'We can see most of the game from here . . . and the sun doesn't get in your eyes.'

I didn't bother to tell him that the leaden clouds meant there would be no sunshine that afternoon. I turned up the collar of the thick coat which my mother insisted I wore; I could feel the beginning of a nasty cold coming on.

The ground gradually filled and the terrace on which we stood soon became crowded.

Not that I minded. Being surrounded by supporters meant being protected from the biting wind. Even so, I began to shiver.

Gareth glanced down in concern. 'Are you all right?'

I nodded. 'Just feeling cold, that's all.'

But he wasn't convinced. 'You don't look well,' he persisted. 'Are you sure you wouldn't like me to take you home?'

'Don't be ridiculous! And miss the game?'

'All right. If you're sure.' He put his arm around me and though it didn't make me feel any warmer, it certainly made me feel good.

But then someone spoke behind us. 'Hi, Gareth. I thought I'd find you here.'

It was Rhiannon. Dressed in tight jeans and a thick

sheepskin jacket that must have cost the earth and wearing a green bobble cap that accentuated the redness of her hair, she looked even more attractive than usual.

Gareth took his arm away and looked around in surprise. 'Thought you said you weren't coming.'

Rhiannon put on all her charm. 'A girl can change her mind, can't she?' she said perkily, putting her arm through Gareth's.

I had the feeling she was doing it for my benefit – as though she were trying to tell me something. So I did the same; put my arm through his. An act which brought a cold look of displeasure to her eyes.

Gareth seemed to enjoy having two girls clinging to him, but as soon as his team jogged on to the field, he shook himself free.

The game was good and fast with plenty of excitement, but though at times I joined in the roars of encouragement, I couldn't really enjoy it. My cold was getting worse. I felt alternately hot and cold, and perspired so much that I could feel my jumper sticking to my skin. The wind gusting through the crowd made me feel bitterly cold.

Not that Gareth noticed. He was much too busy cheering his team to victory.

'Did you see that try?' he yelled at me once above the deep-throated roar of appreciation from the crowd. 'Did you see Griffiths go for the line?'

I tried to share his enthusiasm, but all I craved was the final whistle. And when it eventually came, and the crowd drained towards the several exits, I allowed myself to be sucked along willingly.

When we met outside, Rhiannon was still with us.

'Going to the disco tonight?' she inquired as we

tramped along the side streets, jostling with the homeward-streaming throng.

Gareth shook his head. 'Not tonight. I'm going to Swansea. I'm taking Claire to the Odeon.'

'Oh! I see!' There was a note in Rhiannon's voice that made me glance at her. And what I saw in her eyes convinced me.

That niggling suspicion which had been at the back of my mind was confirmed, and I wondered just how much longer she would remain my friend.

Chapter 9

I didn't go to Swansea that evening after all. Within an hour of arriving home I had begun to shiver so violently that my mother ordered me to bed. I lay under my duvet, hugging my hot water bottle, my head throbbing and pains shooting through my eyes. I was aware, dimly, of my mother phoning Gareth and telling him that I wouldn't be able to go to the cinema after all, and would he apologize to his parents for me.

'But you can call up tomorrow, if you like,' I heard her say.

Oh, great! I thought dismally. Now he'll go to the disco and Rhiannon will get her claws into him. What chance will I have then?

Gradually, I drifted off into a troubled sleep and awoke several times to discover that I'd thrown off my duvet and was lying damp and cold in the freezing darkness.

I didn't feel much better next morning and spent the time wondering if Gareth had gone to the disco after all. But just after lunch – which I couldn't eat – the phone rang and a few minutes later, my mother came running up the stairs to announce that Gareth would be around in half an hour.

'But Mum.' I wailed. 'I can't let him see me like this.'

Though I desperately wanted him to come, I was scared he might not like what he saw.

She stood back, examining me critically. 'You're right. That nose of yours is rather red, and you are looking rather pale . . . '

I sighed despondently.

Then she brightened up. 'But it's surprising what a bit of make-up will do . . . '

I had a quick wash and she spent about ten minutes camouflaging my nose with dabs of face powder and skilfully applying some blusher to my cheeks.

'That's much better,' she said with an encouraging smile. 'He won't believe you're ill at all.'

He arrived just a quarter of an hour later. He walked into the room, looked at me, and stopped dead in his tracks.

'Hey. You look terrible.' he said.

I sat upright in bed. 'Thank you very much. That's all I wanted to hear . . . '

I could have cried.

He ran a hand through his mop of dark hair. 'I didn't mean it . . . not like that, I didn't . . . I mean . . . ' He paused, totally confused.

'What do you mean?' I demanded.

'You look ill . . . ' he began slowly. Then he grinned

'But you still look great.'

Tears began to well up ridiculously into my eyes and I gave a loud sniff. 'Honestly? You really mean it?'

'Of course I do. A heavy cold isn't going to make you any less pretty, is it?'

I wasn't so sure, but his words were sincere, and that was good enough for me. He gave me a box of chocolates and together we ate them and talked. To my relief, I discovered that he hadn't been to the disco after all.

An hour later when he left, though my cold was as bad as ever, I felt much better, and I slipped gently in to a deep slumber where all my dreams were pleasant ones.

I stayed in bed the whole of the next day as well, though the aches had stopped and I was itching to get up. But I was determined to be well enough to go to school on the Thursday to make sure of my place in the team.

Simon phoned on Tuesday evening, dismissed my cold with words of commiseration that lasted at least fifteen seconds and spent the rest of the time talking about his job and how much he was looking forward to going to Biggin Hill. As I listened I thought of what Dawn had said about him and decided she was right: he really was self-centred and conceited. Why hadn't I noticed it before?

But the evening brightened up when Gareth, Steve and Elin appeared out of the blue and we spent another pleasant evening together. My mother, determined not to be eclipsed by Mrs Morgan's culinary prowess, made us a chicken curry for supper.

However, a disappointment awaited me when I returned to school and looked at the notices in the common room. The team for the Saturday game had been pinned on the board, but my name wasn't on it.

'I'm sorry, Claire,' Miss Reynolds apologized when we met in the corridor. 'But I didn't know whether you'd be well enough in time . . . and I really can't change it now, can I? But I'd be very pleased if you could turn out for the practice match after school tonight.'

I went home at lunchtime to get my kit, but had I known what lay in front of me that evening, I don't think I would have been quite so eager to play.

Miss Reynolds placed me alongside Rhiannon as she had the previous week, but this time there were no smiles, just a curious studied indifference which un-nerved me. The game didn't go well either. For some reason, I found myself running all over the place. Rhiannon's passing wasn't as good as it had been earlier; and neither was Jane's. Somehow, they placed the ball just too far in front of me so that more often than not, my marker got to it before me. And when it was accurate, the ball came much too fast and hard so that I had difficulty in controlling it. By half time, I had run myself into the ground.

'What on earth do you think you're playing at?' Rhiannon demanded as we changed sides. 'Why can't you get to the ball?'

'Because you don't pass it properly,' I retorted.

'Oh, don't I?' She breathed indignantly. 'Then how come Elin has no difficulty getting it?'

She was right. Elin was playing well. And then the truth suddenly dawned on me — though at first I couldn't believe it. So during the second half, I paid close attention to her passes. They were very sym-pathetic as far as Elin was concerned, but when either Rhiannon or Jane passed to me, the ball was almost always just too far away.

Rhiannon was an experienced player; her passing was excellent. So it couldn't be an accident. She was deliberately making me play badly – and succeeding.

Then one incident finally convinced me.

Elin and I were tearing up the field, with Rhiannon in possession, when I found myself unmarked just inside the striking circle. Rhiannon saw it too, and flicked the ball towards me. It was a fifty/fifty ball, placed just a few yards to my left. I dashed for it, aware that the goalkeeper was coming out too, narrowing the angle to the goal mouth.

I reached the ball just before her. As I struck it, she went down, her pads before her. I heard a dull thud and through the corner of my eye, saw it deflected behind the goal line. But I was running too fast. I crashed into her and went flying over her head to land in a sickening heap on the ground. For a moment or two, I lay winded as the world went spinning round me.

Then Rhiannon came up. 'Really, Claire,' she said with a concern that didn't fool me at all. 'You must be more careful. You could do yourself an injury like that . . .'

She took my hand, smirked, and pulled me to my feet with a jerk that almost dislocated my shoulder. That fall shook me up and I quivered so much that my game went to pieces. But at least I had one consolation: now I knew exactly where I stood.

We were coming off the field when I noticed that some of the boys who had been playing Rugby on an adjoining pitch had been watching us, among them Gareth. He fell in beside me.

'Hey. Don't take it so badly,' he said, aware of my despondency. 'It wasn't your fault.'

My heart gave a sudden leap. He had seen what had happened; had noticed what Rhiannon had been doing.

'You don't think so?'

But his next words made it plunge. 'Of course not. You were off form, that's all.'

Neither of us had noticed Rhiannon. 'I'm sure that's what it is, Claire,' she said. 'Perhaps you're not feeling well. It can affect your game, you know.'

She was so sympathetic that Gareth was deceived. 'That's right. You'll play better next time . . .'

But Rhiannon hadn't quite finished with me. 'Let's hope Miss Reynolds realizes it,' she added, making me go cold all over. 'I'd hate you to be dropped from the side before you've had a chance to get in.'

It was raining hard next morning and the weatherman had forecast a wet weekend. Which gave me a great deal of satisfaction knowing that the match would probably be cancelled – a thought that made me feel guilty as soon as it occurred to me.

As I walked to the Sixth Form block, Mr Mortimer called me to his office.

'Ah! Claire!' he said, smiling, clapping his hands together and rubbing them. 'Would you do me a favour, please? Jane Watkins is away, so I wonder if you could do her gate duty for her.' He didn't give me a chance to reply. 'Good. Good. I knew I could depend on you.'

So fifteen minutes later, Elin and I were huddled miserably under an umbrella taking the names of latecomers. Except there weren't any. But just as assembly was about to finish, Turner strolled through the gates, hands in pockets, impervious to the rain that plastered his hair to his head.

He had caught me in a foul mood. I stepped in front of him.

'Name?' I demanded.

He looked up, dazed and incredulous. 'What?'

'I asked you what your name was.'

'I know what you said . . . ' A hardness crept into his voice. 'Why?'

'Because you're late . . .and I'm reporting you . . . '

Elin came behind me. 'Leave him alone,' she warned. 'He's trouble . . .'

'I don't care. I'm reporting him.'

A smirk of sheer contempt smeared his face as he thrust it towards me. I could see the blackheads on his flat cheekbones.

'She's right. Anyone reports me is in trouble . . .'

I stepped back, suddenly afraid. 'Do you think I care?'

With a wave of his arm, he swept me roughly aside. 'All right. Go ahead. Try it and see.' Then he swaggered across the yard.

'Oh, Claire. What did you want to do a stupid thing like that for?' Elin was clearly worried. 'You know the sort of reputation he's got. There's no knowing what he'd do. You can't possibly tell Mr Mortimer . . . '

But I did tell Mr Mortimer. 'Turner again?' he bellowed and stormed down the corridor in the direction of the classrooms.

Turner was waiting for me that breaktime. I had my head down, averting my face from the lashing rain as I hurried to the common room, and didn't see him until he barred the way.

'Thought you'd like to know, Miss Bossy-Boots Courtney. I got the stick because of you this morning . . . one on each hand. So like I said; you're for it . . .'

I'd already regretted my actions; not because of his threats, but because I felt sorry for him. I tried to thrust past him but he grabbed my shoulder and spun me round.

'You think you're somebody, don't you? You think because your father's the boss, he's better than my old man, don't you? Well, he isn't. See!' He jabbed me with his finger. 'And you're no better than me . . . for all your posh talk. So remember this. I'm going to get you . . . not now . . . but one day when you're not expecting it. So start worrying.'

Chapter 10

I hadn't seen my father looking so pleased for weeks. He sat opposite me at breakfast, reading a letter which had just arrived, and smiling. My mother placed his bacon and eggs in front of him and glanced over his shoulder.

'Good news?' she inquired.

He nodded. 'It's a letter from our solicitors. We've had an offer for the house.'

I felt my stomach flip over.

'But that's marvellous!' She took the letter and scanned it. Then her face fell. 'Oh . . . it's not as much as we were hoping for, is it?'

'A thousand less to be exact . . .' He looked at my

mother who was now sitting at the head of the table. 'What do you think? Do we take it, or wait until we get a better price?'

She put down the letter with a sigh. 'I don't know. I'm fed up with waiting . . . yet a thousand pounds is a lot of money.'

'True. But the interest on the bridging loan is mounting up'

'So you think we should accept it?' It was more of a statement than a question.

'Yes I do. We don't know when we might get a better offer.'

She thought for a few moments as she sipped her coffee. 'You're right. I think you should phone up the solicitor and tell him we accept.'

I felt dejected as I listened to them. Not once had they asked my opinion . . . and the fact that one more link with home was being broken made me feel sad. Especially after what had happened the previous day.

Even though it was Saturday, Dad went to work so Mum suggested we went to Swansea for the day.

'We haven't been there yet,' she pointed out. 'And since I haven't bought you anything new for ages, I think it's time I did, don't you?'

I immediately perked up. 'That's fantastic. When are we going?'

My mother laughed. 'As soon as you're ready,' she said.

We were on the road within half an hour. She drove into Pencarnog, went straight ahead at the traffic lights towards the industrial park where Dad worked. I thought of him as we drove past. He'd been working long hours recently and it didn't seem fair that he had to work on Saturday mornings as well. Half an hour later, we were driving into the centre of Swansea, though we had twice lost our way and were entering it from the oppsite direction.

'Look out for the Dragon Hotel,' Mum advised as she drove cautiously through the city. 'Mrs Evans tells me there's a car park nearby.'

As we approached a large roundabout, I saw it: a large brick building with four emblems on the front and a six-storeyed central tower. At the same moment, I saw the familiar National Car Park sign — black initials on a yellow background. 'There's the car park. Take the third exit . . . '

Minutes later, we had parked on the fifth floor of the multi-storey car park, and were walking out into a watery sunlight. Swansea was a pleasant surprise. Though most of it was built on surrounding hills, the city centre itself was on the narrow plain that ended at the sea and had wide open streets. There were large department stores as well as smaller shops.

My mother consulted a rough map which Mrs Evans had drawn. 'We must make our way to the Quadrant. If we go down the Kingsway and turn left, we should find it.'

'The Quadrant?'

'It's a shopping precinct,' she explained. 'That's where we'll find Debenham's as well as those fashion shops you're dying to get into . . . '

We didn't arrive there until almost an hour later. There were so many stores on the way which were much too exciting to pass, that it was just before eleven when we walked into the mall with its avenue of shops.

I still hadn't bought anything two hours later when Mum insisted on lunching at the Dragon Hotel.

We found a table near a window overlooking the

roundabout. As we ate, we watched the world go by, cars and buses and an ever thickening mass of shoppers. Mum wondered what it would be like at Christmas. I couldn't wait to go round the shops again. We went to three more department stores before deciding on a tightly fitting polo-necked jumper in lambswool and a pair of stretch jeans.

'And now,' Mum said with a sigh of relief. 'Let's go home. My feet are killing me . . . '

But instead of going directly home, she made a tour of Pencarnog, driving slowly along the streets which radiated from the central traffic lights. She kept glancing quickly from side to side as she passed the rows of shops.

'What on earth are you looking for, Mum,' I said in exasperation as she pulled into a parking place.

She switched off the engine and stared thoughtfully in front of her. 'If I'm not mistaken, there's not a single boutique in Pencarnog, at least not one that might cater exclusively for young people.'

'So?'

'So there's a need for one . . . '

'But there are several in Swansea,' I pointed out.

'Exactly. And it costs money to get there, doesn't it?'

I looked at her suspiciously. 'Surely you're not thinking of opening one here?'

'Why not?'

'But it's so small . . . there aren't enough people . . .'

She shook her head. 'That's where you're wrong. Did you know that over thirty-five thousand people live in Pencarnog alone . . . that's not counting the outlying villages. You've seen it on market day. It's absolutely heaving . . . '

'But what about the one Mrs Metcalfe's looking

after for you?'

She breathed a deep sigh. 'I'm going to have to sell that, Claire. I think we're going to have to accept the fact that Pencarnog is going to be our home for a long time yet.'

Her words depressed me. Deep down, I'd always thought that in time, we'd all move back nearer London.

'So . . . ' She switched on the engine. 'It's time I thought of opening another one.'

Robert's car was in the drive when we arrived home and Mum gave a shriek of delight.

'My boy's come home,' she cried. 'My baby boy's come home.'

I actually winced. If she behaved like that in front of Gareth or the others, I'd die.

'Oh, Mum.' I protested in my most grown-up voice. 'Do you have to behave in that ridiculous manner?'

But she wasn't listening. She had scrambled out of the car and was rushing into the house, and when I walked into the living-room where Robert had been watching Grandstand on television, she was hugging him. Robert, of course, was struggling to get free – without much success – but despite his protests, I had the distinct feeling that he was enjoying it all.

I shook my head in incredulity. Mothers. I thought. Some daughters do have them!

But as I stood at the door and watched them – Dad grinning with a glass of whisky in his hand, and Robert trying to push his dishevelled hair back into place – I realized with a strange kind of sadness that we were all together again. Something I had missed without being aware of it.

It must have been an hour later before Robert and I

had a chance to talk. I had taken him to show him my room and he whistled his admiration.

'You're lucky, you know . . . ' He was standing at the window, gazing out at the rear garden, 'this room's much bigger than mine . . . and the view . . . '

'The view's not everything,' I said sullenly.

He turned round. 'Do I detect a sign that someone's not too happy here?'

I gave a quick shrug of my shoulders. 'You can say that again.'

'I see. Fancy talking about it?'

'What's the use? What good will it do?'

He walked to the settee and sat down. 'You never know. It might help.'

I looked at him undecidedly. I dearly wanted to talk to someone about Rhiannon and the way things had deteriorated between us. I couldn't confide in Gareth and I wasn't sure how my mother would react, seeing how friendly she and Mrs Evans had become. But Robert, I knew, was different. He'd understand. So, hesitantly at first, and then with growing confidence as anger and indignation made me fluent, I told him everything.

He listened without interruption and when I'd finished, there was a long silence.

'This Rhiannon . . . ' he said pensively, 'she doesn't seem a nice character, does she?'

I frowned. 'She can be very nice . . . ' I desperately wanted to be fair to her. 'She was at the beginning. We got on really well . . . until she discovered that Gareth preferred me to her.'

Robert grinned. 'And what about Simon?'

I felt my face go red. 'What about him? He's over a hundred miles away . . . ' I realized he was goading me.

'Besides, as you once said, we all have to make new friends some day . . . '

He laughed and pushed himself to his feet. 'I asked for that, didn't I? But what are you going to do about Rhiannon?'

'What can I do? I'll have to grin and bear it, I suppose. And hope that things will improve . . . '

He put his arm round my shoulder and led me to the door. 'Don't let her get you down; that's the important thing. And now, I think we'd better go down to tea.'

As we ate, my father was very quiet, so withdrawn and preoccupied that he might just as well have been in another room. He was the same later when we watched television.

In the end, my mother's patience was exhausted; she rose to her feet and switched off the television. We all looked up in surprise.

'Now then, Derrick!' she said firmly. 'Something's worrying you and I want to know what it is.'

Dad looked at her and frowned. 'Is it that obvious?'

'Obvious? If you were sitting where I was you'd know.'

'I see . . . ' He thought for a moment. 'Well . . . if you must know. I had a visit from Head Office this morning.'

'On a Saturday?'

'Particularly on a Saturday. They wanted to make a tour of the place . . . while the workmen weren't around.'

My mother was mystified. 'But why?'

Dad leaned forward. 'If I tell you, then you must promise me one thing: it won't go out of this room.' He looked around at Robert and me. 'I'm including you two in this. Especially you, Claire.'

We all looked at one another. 'Well, go on.' Mum said impatiently. 'You've got our promise. What are you trying to tell us?'

He paused before speaking. 'It's like this. As you know, the factory has been making a loss for some time, and one of the things I had to do was find out why and try to correct it.'

'And have you? Found out why'

He nodded gravely. 'It didn't take a genius to do that. We don't have a big enough share of the market and the workforce is too large.'

I think we all knew what was coming next.

'Which means we're going to have some redundancies.'

I just couldn't keep quiet. 'But that's terrible, Dad. If you sack these people where else are they going to find work?'

'That's what's worrying me. We're the biggest employer in the area . . . and any redundancies are going to hit Pencarnog badly. Of course, I'm hoping to make them voluntary, if we can get enough of the older men to retire prematurely, it will ease the problem . . . and the company's agreed to be generous. But . . . '

He raised his hands in a gesture of helplessness.

We were all silent, but then Robert spoke and he voiced the thought that must have been in all our minds.

'Whatever happens,' he said simply. 'It's not going to make us very popular, is it?'

Chapter 11

For the whole of the week leading up to half-term, Rhiannon conducted a whispering campaign against me. Whenever I approached her, she'd start speaking in Welsh, and it was obvious from the amused glances the other girls gave that she was talking about me. I noticed that it embarrassed Elin very much.

I must admit she was very cunning about it; she never did it when Gareth was around.

On the Friday afternoon, however, something happened which made me appreciate just how far she was prepared to go to make me unpopular.

In the game of hockey Miss Reynolds had placed me in the opposing team to Rhiannon's, and during the first half, the game went well. Several times, I was able to outmanoeuvre most of her team and I was not only glad that I hadn't lost my form, but the shouts of praise from Miss Reynolds made me very pleased with myself.

It was during the second half that things went wrong. Elin had passed the ball to Rhiannon who was dribbling up the centre of the field. I fell back, determined to stop her as she drove towards the goalmouth. As I got near, she looked round, and then, just as I caught up with her, she did the most amazing thing.

She launched herself into the air, landed with a thud

on the grass and slithered through the mud.

I couldn't believe it had happened. I looked down at her, dimly aware that a whistle had been blown. Miss Reynolds ran across the field.

'What on earth do you think you're playing at?' she demanded angrily. 'How dare you employ such disgraceful tactics on this field?'

'But Miss . . . I didn't . . .'

'Don't argue with me . . . you can get off . . . right now . . .'

She turned to Rhiannon who was already levering herself off the ground. 'Are you all right?'

'But Miss,' I protested in disbelief. 'I didn't do a thing . . .'

'Didn't do a thing?' Her voice had a ring of contempt. 'You'll be telling me next that she tripped . . .'

'But that's . . .'

'No.' The word exploded from her lips. 'No, Claire Courtney. I saw it with my own eyes. It was a deliberate foul . . . and I'm not going to stand for it. Now get back to the changing room and wait until I arrive.'

The other girls had gathered round and I could feel their hostility towards me. Though I was innocent, I walked away in shame, back to the changing room, feeling so sick that I thought I was going to be ill. Though I'd often heard of players taking a fall just to save a game that wasn't the reason Rhiannon had done it. But even so I couldn't believe that she'd really go that far.

Some time later when the others returned no one said a word to me. Then Miss Reynolds came marching in.

'Get changed quickly,' she ordered, the anger still in

her voice. 'Claire Courtney. I'll see you in my room . . . Now!'

I followed her into a small changing room, complete with its private shower. Items of equipment were scattered in an untidy heap in one corner.

'Close the door!' she commanded, spinning round as soon as I'd done so. 'I'd like an explanation of that incident, if you don't mind . . . ' Typically, she didn't give me a chance to reply. 'I haven't been so disgusted in my life.'

'But Miss . . .'

'Be quiet. I am appalled. I don't know if that's the sort of behaviour they allowed in your previous school, but it's not going to happen here . . . '

Though tears were already brimming in my eyes – tears of anger and frustration at the injustice of what was happening – I couldn't take it lying down.

'I didn't do anything!' I blurted out.

Miss Reynold's eyes hardened. 'You'll say "Miss" when you address me, girl . . . even if you are in the Sixth Form.' She leaned forward, hands aggressively on her hips, staring right into my eyes. 'Do you think I'm blind? Do you think I didn't see you hook your stick around Rhiannon's foot?'

Oh, what's the use? I thought, turning my head away. I could see she wasn't going to believe anything I said. I was guilty; it had already been decided.

Then there came a knock on the door.

'Who is it?' she snapped.

The door opened and Rhiannon appeared.

'Please, Miss . . . ' she said meekly. 'May I see you for a minute?' Without waiting for a reply, she came in and half closed the door behind her. 'I wanted to see you about, Claire, Miss. I'm sure she didn't mean to do it. I'm sure it was an accident . . . '

Miss Reynolds said nothing for a moment, and in the silence, I could hear the muffled whispers of girls who had obviously gathered outside the door to listen. She pulled herself up, took a deep breath and looked at us both.

'It's very generous of you to say so, Rhiannon . . . '

'And there's no damage done . . . I haven't even pulled a muscle.'

Again there was that silence as she considered what Rhiannon had said.

'Very well . . . if you can forgive her, then I'm sure I can.'

Rhiannon smiled and left.

'And you, Miss,' she said, turning to me, 'can consider yourself very fortunate. I think you'd better go . . . before I change my mind . . . '

I walked the few steps to the door. Then she called me back.

'Claire Courtney,' she said. 'You have the makings of a good player . . . a very good player. But if you're going to employ the tactics I've witnessed this afternoon, then I'm afraid you haven't a chance of playing in any of my teams. I suggest you think seriously about what I've said.'

I returned to the changing room to pick up my bag and found Elin waiting for me. I was glad that the others had left because I could imagine the reception I would have received.

'Oh, Elin!' I sat down wearily and put my hands over my face. 'I didn't do it . . . honestly I didn't. She deliberately threw herself on the ground . . . '

'I know!' Elin said quietly.

For a moment, I thought I hadn't heard properly.

Then I looked up. 'You know?'

She nodded. 'I was a few yards behind you. I saw exactly what happened.'

I breathed a sigh of relief. 'Thank goodness for that. Do you know? I was beginning to believe I was guilty . . . that I had actually done it . . . '

Then the realization struck home that if she knew, why hadn't she told Miss Reynolds? The look I gave her was enough.

'I know what you're going to say,' she went on quickly. 'Why didn't I tell Miss Reynolds?' She shrugged her shoulders helplessly. 'I don't know. I was scared I expect . . . not that Rhiannon would get her own back . . .not physically, I mean . . .I suppose I didn't think anyone would believe me . . . I'm sorry . . . '

She looked so contrite that I couldn't do anything but forgive her. 'Forget it, Elin!' I said, putting my hand on her arm. 'It doesn't really matter. Just as long as we're friends . . . '

At that moment, Miss Reynolds walked through the changing room. As she glanced at us, there was a puzzled concerned look in her eyes and I could have sworn she was going to say something. Then she changed her mind. With a curt 'goodnight, girls', she stepped through the outer door into the yard.

I was still angry when I met Gareth outside the school gates not five minutes later. He'd showered and his hair was sleeked back over his head. He watched me cautiously as I approached.

'Hi!' he said, trying to smile. 'Everything all right?'

I glanced at him coldly. 'Why shouldn't it be . . . ?'

'No reason. I just thought . . . '

'You thought what?'

'Nothing.' For once he was at a loss for words.

I looked straight at him. 'Look Gareth. Why don't you tell me what's on your mind? You've heard what happened on the field, haven't you?'

He ran a hand through his hair. 'Yeah ... I have ... '

'And you'd like to know why I did it?' I didn't give him a chance to reply. 'What if I told you I didn't do it? Suppose I said Rhiannon threw herself on the ground ...?'

'I'd believe you ... I suppose ... '

'Suppose? You don't sound very sure.'

I turned and walked away and he had to run to catch up.

'Hold on, Claire. I am sure. It's just that I can't understand why she should do such a thing ... '

I stopped dead in my tracks. 'Oh, Gareth. Are you stupid or something? Because of you, of course ... '

'Me?' He was totally mystified and his lack of insight angered me. 'What's it got to do with me?'

'Look, Gareth!' I said in exasperation. 'Why don't you ask Elin. Perhaps she'll tell you ... because I can't. And now ... will you stop following me ... I want to be alone ... '

I turned and ran up the road wishing I'd never come to live in Pencarnog.

But when I arrived home, my mother had the perfect solution – even if it was only a temporary one.

'I phoned Mrs Metcalfe this afternoon,' she said, pouring out a cup of tea. 'I've arranged to stay with her for a few days ... you can come too if you like.'

'If I like?' It was the answer to my prayer. 'When are

we leaving?'

'Tonight, as soon as your father arrives home,' she said.

I couldn't wait. I wanted to get as far away from Pencarnog as possible.

Chapter 12

It was almost eleven o'clock before we pulled up outside Mrs Metcalfe's house. And not a moment too soon. The journey had dragged as I willed my mother to drive faster so that I could get there in time to phone Simon. But since it was so late, my mother didn't think it wise and reluctantly, I took her advice.

Mrs Metcalfe was really pleased to see us. 'You've changed,' she said, looking me up and down carefully. 'In just a few weeks you've become quite the young lady. And do I detect just a trace of a Welsh accent?' she asked with a laugh.

She had prepared a light supper and by the time we'd unpacked it was ready on the table. But I was tired and soon after, I went to bed. I took out a book and tried to read, but I couldn't concentrate. I kept thinking of Dad and Pencarnog – but most of all I thought of Gareth and began to regret having lost my temper.

In the end, I threw the book on the floor, put out the light and snuggled into my pillow.

The next morning was bright and sharp with the

unmistakable tang of autumn in the air. As I looked out of my bedroom window into the large rear garden, I noticed a faint powdering of frost on the grass, and knew without having to go out that it was much colder there than in Pencarnog. I shivered in spite of the central heating, and jumped back into bed until I heard Mrs Metcalfe moving about below.

As soon as breakfast was over, I phoned Simon. I heard his sleepy voice at the other end of the line. 'Hello,' I said. 'It's me . . . Claire . . .'

'Claire?' His voice sounded muffled.

'You know. The girl you said you'd always love . . . '

'Oh, that Claire.'

I wasn't sure whether he was joking or not. 'Yes . . . that Claire.'

'How strange. I was going to phone you this afternoon.'

'Just as well you didn't.'

'Oh, why not?'

'Because I'm not in Penarnog. I'm here . . . '

'Here?' He sounded bewildered now.

'At Mrs Metcalfe's. Mum and I have come home for the weekend.'

There was a moment's silence.

'No kidding? You're here . . . actually here?'

'That's right . . . just half a mile away . . . '

'But that's fantastic . . ' Now there was excitement in his voice. 'When am I going to see you?'

'Right now if you like.'

'Great. I'll . . .' Then he gave a groan. 'Oh, no. I forgot. I'm going into work today . . .'

'I see . . .' I felt my heart plummet. To think I'd come all this way only to discover that he was working.

'But we'll be able to go out tonight,' he went on. 'Tell

you what. Remember that night we had at the Swan? We can go there . . . have a basket meal . . . then go to the disco. What do you say?'

'That will be great,' I said, though my enthusiasm had been dampened.

'It's a date then. I'll pick you up at half-past seven. O.K.? But look. I've got to dash . . .I'm late . . . don't want to get the sack.'

In typical fashion, he slammed the phone down and I was left holding a dead receiver.

Mum and Mrs Metcalfe left to go to the shop having arranged to meet for lunch at one. Left on my own, I phoned Dawn and went through the same ritual of bewilderment and disbelief.

'Why don't you come round?' she suggested. 'Though give me another half hour. I haven't washed yet . . . let alone had breakfast.'

I decided to give her at least an hour. I spent the time washing up the breakfast dishes and listening to Radio One. Most of my excitement had evaporated, though some of it returned when Dawn greeted me like a long-lost friend. She chattered incessantly as she made coffee – mostly about how she and Julian had had this quarrel and now she had a new boyfriend called Roddy.

'But tell me what Wales is like?' she said as she carried the tray into the lounge.

Her question made me think. 'It's all right, I suppose. Not a bit like here . . . and not a bit like I expected either.'

'Sounds intriguing.'

I smiled at her. 'It's quite beautiful . . . in a wild rugged sort of way. I thought there'd be coal-mines all over the place, but I haven't seen one yet. I must ask

Gareth to take me to see one.'

'Gareth . . .' She leaned forward excitedly. 'Who's he?'

'Just a fella in the Sixth Form,' I said airily.

'Just a fella . . . come off it, Claire Courtney. You can't fool me. I can smell a romance, a mile away . . .'

'This one's over a hundred miles away,' I pointed out.

'I don't care. I want to know what he's like.'

'Well . . .' I began 'He is rather nice . . . and we do get on well together.'

'Ho! Ho!' Her eyes were full of mischief. 'What's Simon going to say when he finds out?'

'What can he say?' I shuffled uncomfortably in my chair. 'We're just friends. There's no law against that.'

'Perhaps not. But he's still mad about you.'

'Is he?' All he ever seemed to talk about on the phone was himself – or the R.A.F.

'I should say so. For weeks, he's been mooning about like a sick cow. And whenever we meet – which thank goodness isn't often – he asks about you. It gets me down.'

'Thanks a lot. Now I know who my friends are.'

Dawn wrinkled up her nose. 'I didn't mean it like that, stupid. I just mean the way he goes on and on and on . . .'

I decided to change the subject. 'And what about you? What's this new boyfriend like?'

'Roddy?' She went misty-eyed. 'Oh, Claire. He really is something. He's a lot older than me . . . he's almost twenty . . .'

'Twenty?' Almost an old-age pensioner, I thought.

'Mmm . . . and he's got this sports car . . . and . . . Oh, Claire. I'm sure it's the real thing this time . . .'

She was beginning to get me down. 'And when am I going to meet the fabulous Roddy? Tonight at the disco?'

She shook her head. 'Sorry, Claire . . . he's taking me to London. To a theatre . . .and dinner afterwards.'

'So I won't be seeing you tonight.'

'Nor this afternoon, I'm afraid. I'm going to see my grandfather, you know; the one in Oxford. But I will be able to see you tomorrow,' she went on hurriedly. 'At least . . . tomorrow morning. His mother's asked me to come to tea tomorrow afternoon. Isn't it great?'

Just great! I thought. What on earth was I going to do with all the spare time.

I spent the whole morning with Dawn, listening with growing irritation as she prattled on about her precious Roddy. I was glad when I had to leave to meet my mother.

We had lunch in a pizza parlour where to my disappointment, she announced that she wouldn't be able to come shopping with me as she'd planned, because she had several things to discuss with Mrs Metcalfe. So I went around on my own.

It wasn't the same; something was missing. And it took me some time to realize what it was. I walked around all afternoon without meeting anyone I knew. Had I been shopping in Pencarnog, I'd have bumped into at least half a dozen friends and there was no way I would have felt so utterly lonely.

Later, out of sheer desperation, I walked from the town centre and strolled along the old familiar streets until I came to Hilltop Close and stood briefly outside our old house. The estate agent's board had 'Sold' printed across it. Curiously, it looked much smaller than I remembered and the rose beds which my father had tended so lovingly had become choked with weeds.

I turned and hurried back down the road with tears stinging my eyes. It wasn't my home any more.

Bored and depressed, I went back to Mrs Metcalfe's house and let myself in. The house was cold and since I didn't know how to turn on the central heating, I had to huddle in front of an electric fire for about half an hour before I warmed up.

As I stared miserably at the glowing bar, I gave myself a mental shake. Snap out of it, Claire Courtney, I told myself sternly; you'll feel better when Simon takes you out tonight.

But I didn't.

Just after six, a heavy drizzle settled down and by half-past seven had developed into teeming rain. I'd imagined us sitting under the fairy lights as we had that night we celebrated our 'O'-level results. It was stupid of me. I should have known we couldn't have sat out in the open at the end of October.

Instead, we were squashed in a corner of an over-crowded room, wet and uncomfortable, with Simon talking incessantly about the R.A.F. and how good his promotion prospects were. After about half an hour I was ready to scream.

Even the disco proved to be a damp squib – which is exactly how I must have looked after we'd walked half a mile through a downpour. I was glad when it was eleven o'clock and I could reasonably make an excuse to go home.

Simon's face fell. 'Do you have to go?'

'I'm afraid so . . . ' I felt rotten as I lied to him. 'Mum especially asked me not to be too late. She doesn't like to keep Mrs Metcalfe up.'

Reluctantly, he took me home. 'Shall I see you tomorrow?' he asked as we stood outside the door.

'I'm not sure . . .' I just couldn't look at him. 'You see . . . Mum said we might be going home early . . .'

'Oh . . .'

'I could phone you if we don't go . . .'

I could tell he didn't believe me. 'Yeah . . . yeah. That will be all right. Give me a call.'

And when he left, he didn't even try to kiss me.

Strangely, we *did* go home early. Before I went to see Dawn next morning, my mother asked me if I minded going back to Wales a day earlier; she was missing Dad.

I shook my head. 'I'm missing him too,' I admitted.

I didn't stay long at Dawn's house and half an hour later, she walked me to the end of the road.

'When am I going to see you next?' she asked.

'I'm not sure . . . you could come and see me if you like . . .'

She nodded and smiled, though there were tears in her eyes. 'That would be nice. I'm looking forward to seeing this Gareth Morgan. I have the feeling he's something special . . .'

'Yes, Dawn,' I said simply. 'I think he is . . .'

Within two hours, we'd had lunch, said goodbye to Mrs Metcalfe, and were speeding along the motorway. Suddenly, Mum turned to me.

'By the way, Claire. I haven't told you. I've sold the business. To Mrs Metcalfe . . .'

I wasn't surprised. I'd suspected that was the reason for our visit.

'Still . . . I'm sure it was nice seeing all your friends again.'

I shrugged my shoulders. 'It was all right . . . but I'm

glad to be going home . . .'

It was at least thirty seconds before she spoke. 'Do you realize what you've just said?' She glanced in my direction, took my hand and squeezed it. 'You've just called Pencarnog home.'

Chapter 13

Dad looked worried when he greeted us and as I took my suitcase to my room, I heard him and Mum arguing in the hall.

'But how did they find out?' she said. 'I didn't breathe a word.'

'Don't ask me, but somebody did . . . or they made a pretty accurate guess . . .'

I didn't take much notice because I was debating whether or not to phone Gareth, but when Mum called me down, it was obvious from Dad's frown that something serious was troubling him.

He didn't mince words. 'Claire. That business about redundancies I told you about . . . You didn't happen to mention it to anyone, did you?'

'Oh, Dad.' His lack of trust hurt me. 'As if I would. I gave you my promise.

'All right. I believe you. I just had to make sure, that's all.'

I glanced at them both. 'Why? What's happened?'

My mother started to speak, but Dad interrupted

her. 'No need to worry Claire about it. Besides it was certain to come out sooner or later.' He brushed a hand in a distracted way through his hair. 'I just wish it had been later, that's all.'

He walked to the door, then turned. 'Oh, by the way. That young man of yours . . . Gareth. He called round about an hour ago . . .'

'Oh, Dad. Why didn't you tell me?'

'Sorry . . . I forgot . . . I told him you'd be home about eight.'

I wasn't listening. I was already on my way to the phone. But it was his mother who answered.

'I'm afraid he's not here,' she said. 'He left the house about ten minutes ago . . . I'm almost sure he said he was on his way to see you . . .'

That was all I needed to know. I grabbed my coat from the cloakroom and dashed out of the house. I couldn't see any sign of him as I hurried down the road. Except for some boys standing at the bottom of the hill where the road from his estate joined ours, the pavement was empty. For a moment, I thought he could be one of them, but as I approached, I could see he wasn't. Though one of them seemed familiar.

It was Turner – with a few of his friends. He looked over his shoulder as I entered the circle of light from the lamp-post under which they were standing, and a malicious smirk crossed his face.

'Well, look who it is! Miss Hoity-Toity herself.'

I ignored him and tried to walk past. But Turner swiftly stood in front of me, barring my way.

'Hold on. You're not going anywhere,' he said menacingly.

I began to get frightened, but there was no way I was going to show him. 'Do you mind?' I said. 'I want to get past . . . '

He laughed and turned to the others. 'Did you hear that? She wants to get past . . .'

As if in response to a hidden signal, they began to encircle me, forcing me to retreat to a low stone wall.

'Not until we've had a talk to you. Not until we've told you what we think of you . . . and your old man.'

I gulped. 'My father? What's it got to do with him?'

They all laughed at my words. 'Did you hear that? What's it got to do with her father?' Turner stopped laughing and thrust his face right up against mine. 'I'll tell you what it's got to do with your father . . . everything.'

I was getting scared now – really scared – especially when Turner smiled at me.

'I think we ought to teach her a lesson, don't you, fellas? Perhaps her father will get the message then. Perhaps he'll know just what we think of him.'

In spite of my fear, I realized just how ridiculous it was – like a scene out of a Western movie and any moment I was expecting the 'this town ain't big enough for both of us' routine.

Then, out of the corner of my eye, I saw a vague shadowy figure appear on the fringe of the circle of light. And then that figure spoke.

'Just lay one finger on her, Turner . . . and I'll mash you into pulp.'

I breathed a huge sigh of relief as I recognized Gareth's voice and saw him walk towards us. Turner spun round, a slight figure in contrast to Gareth; but in spite of the difference in size, he still possessed the bully's blind courage.

'You going to take on all of us?' he asked contemptuously.

'If I have to . . . yes.' His voice was quiet, but the threat was clear.

He took a step towards Turner and as he did so, the others backed away, so that only Turner stood challenging him. Turner glanced apprehensively over his shoulder, aware suddenly that he was on his own. Fear flickered in his eyes.

Gareth came right up to him, and this time, it was Turner's turn to have a face thrust against his.

'Think the others are going to help you?' He looked up, over Turner's shoulder at the huddle of boys grouped together in a vain attempt to gain courage from each other. 'I suggest you lot clear off. I just want to talk to Turner.'

One by one, they slunk silently away. Gareth turned back to Turner prodding him with his finger, forcing him back. 'I'm not going to threaten you, Turner . . . I'm just making a promise. If you as much as come near Claire . . . let alone touch her . . . you'll wish you hadn't been born. Now . . . I suggest you join your friends . . . ' But Turner was defiant. He stood up to Gareth.

For a moment, I thought there was going to be a fight.

'Fancy your chances?' Gareth's voice was calm. 'If you're going to do something, you'd better do it soon. Either have a go at me . . . or join your friends . . . '

Turner had second thoughts. He turned sharply and walked away, hands in his pockets as he swaggered down the road. But when he reached the others, he turned.

'You just watch it, Morgan,' he yelled, the contempt back in his voice. 'We'll get you one day . . . '

Gareth spun round and did one of his standing

sprints. The gang tried to scatter. But all they managed to do was get tangled up with one another, landing in a sprawling heap on the ground.

Gareth laughed at them. 'Just you try it. Any time.'

Strangely, as I watched them slink foolishly away, I felt sorry for them, in spite of the way they had threatened me. With a guy like Gareth around they didn't stand a chance. And they knew it.

He came back, hands thrust deeply into the pockets of his duffel coat. 'Lucky I came along,' he said with a wry grin.

'You can say that again . . . ' My heart was still thumping against my ribs. 'My fault. I shouldn't have reported him. Though I can't understand why he brought my father into it? What has it got to do with him?'

Gareth looked at me curiously. 'You mean you don't know?'

'Know what?'

'About the report in Saturday's *Clarion* . . . '

The *Pencarnog Clarion* was the local evening paper. I shook my head. 'Should I?'

'There was a report about your father's factory . . . hit the headlines. It said there were going to be redundancies.'

I gasped. 'So that was why dad was worried.'

'You knew about it?'

Now that it was common knowledge, there was no purpose in denying it. 'Dad mentioned it some time ago . . . '

'So it's true. No wonder Turner was annoyed.'

I shook my head in bewilderment. 'Hold on. These redundancies . . . they're just a possibility. They might never happen. And anyway; what's it got to do with

Turner? He doesn't work at the factory . . . '

'No. But his father does.' Gareth led me back along the road to my house. 'And if there are redundancies, he might lose his job. It's not funny, Claire . . . '

I sighed deeply. 'I know it isn't. But why blame me?'

'It's his way of getting back at your father,' he explained. 'I know it's stupid, but people are worried . . . there's been a lot of hot air spoken . . . and Turner's heard it all. Anyway you were lucky I came along. What were you doing out alone?'

'I was coming to meet you.' I told him how I'd phoned his home and spoken to his mother. 'And . . . and I wanted to apologize.'

'Apologize? What for?'

'For being so horrible last Friday. I can't blame you for not believing what I said . . . '

'But I do believe you,' he protested. 'I did at the time.'

'You did?'

He put his arm round my shoulder. 'Of course. I just couldn't understand all that business about me and Rhiannon . . . it didn't make sense. So I did what you suggested and asked Elin.'

'Oh!' It was something I hoped he wouldn't do. 'And she told you?'

He nodded his head slowly. 'I found it incredible. I've always liked Rhiannon . . . I've known her since we were in the primary school together . . .but . . . I've always regarded her as a sister . . . never as a girl-friend.'

'She obviously doesn't look upon you as a brother . . . which is why she was so hurt.' We had reached home by now and stood together in the darkness of the porch. 'If it happened to me, I'd have been hurt too. . . '

'Would you?'

'Of course!'

He turned me to face him. 'Look, Claire. You must know how I feel about you. I . . . I'd like you to be my girl . . . if you don't mind . . .'

'Oh, Gareth.' My eyes misted over with happiness. 'Of course I don't mind.'

He took me into his arms and kissed me, a slow, gentle, lingering kiss that left me breathless and dizzy.

'By the way!' he whispered. 'Wales are playing England soon . . at the National Stadium in Cardiff . . . do you fancy coming with me?'

I nodded and laughed in a soft amused way. It was, I knew an even greater compliment than inviting me to watch Pencarnog Rugby Football Club on a miserable Saturday afternoon.

Chapter 14

A pleasant surprise awaited me when I returned to school after half term. Miss Reynolds called me to her room after morning assembly and told me that she'd thought about what had happened before the holidays and decided, since it could quite possibly have been an accident as Rhiannon had suggested, to include me in the first team for the next match.

'But please, Claire. I don't want anything like that happening again.'

Deciding to let sleeping dogs lie, I promised her that it wouldn't.

I walked out to find Elin waiting for me. 'What did she want?' she asked anxiously.'

'She's changed her mind. She's picked me for the first team.'

Elin broke into a wide smile. 'That's fantastic . . . though I'm not surprised. You've been playing well recently.'

We walked together across the yard. 'But why? What happened to make her change her mind . . . that's what I'd like to know. Do you think she heard us talking . . . when she walked through the changing room?'

'Does it matter?'

I shrugged my shoulders. 'Not really. But I can't help wondering what Rhiannon's reaction is going to be. After all, if we have to play together, it would be better if we were friends . . . '

I didn't have to wait long. The team was posted up on the notice-board before break and Rhiannon was furious. Coldly furious. Her dark eyes flashed with anger when I walked into the common room, and though she didn't say anything, my heart sank. I couldn't help wondering where it was all going to end, because I knew that neither of us could go on like this for much longer.

My mother too was bubbling over with excitement when I arrived home that evening.

'I've got some news . . . good news.' she announced, hardly able to contain her pleasure. 'I'm going to open a boutique in Pencarnog.'

'You are? Where?'

As she poured the tea, she looked at me across the

table. 'Do you remember the day we went to Swansea?'

'And you drove slowly round Pencarnog afterwards . . . '

'That's right.' She took a small sip of tea. 'Well, the next day, I took a walk round the town and found just what I was looking for . . . an empty shop.'

'But where?' I couldn't think of any.

'Not far from the market. It's in a side street that leads down to the river.'

Then I remembered. 'Not the one next to that sports shop?'

I could visualize it in my mind: small, dirty, cobwebs in the window and flaking brown paint.

'That's it. The sports shop already attracts people . . . just what I want . . . '

I stared at her in amazement. 'But Mum. It's grotty . . . '

'It is at the moment.' My criticism did nothing to dampen her enthusiasm. 'But it won't be. Not after I've finished with it. Of course, I shall need some help. There's Gareth for a start.'

'You're not going to ask my friends?' I wailed.

'Why not? I shall pay them. I'm sure they'll be only too pleased to earn some pocket money for Christmas.'

My mother was in one of her organizing moods and nothing was going to deflect her from her purpose.

'When are you going to start?' I asked dejectedly.

'I have to wait first to see if my offer is accepted. Frankly they were asking too much and I told them so. And then I'll have to wait until the money from Mrs Metcalfe comes through . . . ' She was looking out of the window, but her mind was as far away as the distant hills. 'I'm wondering about using Welsh fabric in my designs. You know . . . that beautiful weave

117

with the traditional geometric pattern. I think I could do something with that . . . ' Then she came down to earth. 'Well . . . we can't sit around and dream all day, can we? Come and help me get your father's meal ready.'

I groaned silently. She really was in one of her organizing moods.

Robert phoned that night.

'Oh, it's you!' I said, thinking it might have been Gareth.

'Thank you for sounding so happy . . .' His voice crackled in the distance. 'And how's that mad rugby-playing boyfriend of yours?'

I told him to mind his own business and he laughed. 'What are you phoning about?' I asked him cheekily. 'Run out of money again?'

'Me run of money? Whatever gave you that idea? As a matter of fact, I thought I'd better warn Mum I'll be home this weekend. I'm going to watch England beat Wales at Cardiff first . . . '

'You are? I exclaimed. 'So am I. Perhaps we could meet.'

'Good idea. Say . . . outside the Angel Hotel at one?'

'Where's the Angel Hotel?'

'You can't miss it. It's almost opposite the Stadium. Now put Mother on the phone, will you? I've only got tenpence left.'

As the week went by, the excitement grew and the only topic in the common room as far as the boys were concerned was the International. I came in for a lot of friendly ribbing since I was the only person there likely to support England that day. Rhiannon, thankfully, kept a discreet silence, and I was relieved that the other girls had forgotten the incident on the hockey pitch.

'Of course, we could give you temporary Welsh citizenship,' Gareth teased as we walked along the riverside walk late that Friday night. 'Until you are a naturalized Welshwoman, of course.'

'Thank you very much. And how long is that likely to take?'

'About forty or fifty years . . . or until you marry some mad Welshman.'

'And what if I don't want to marry some mad Welshman?' I put the emphasis on the word 'mad'.

He stopped and turned. 'That's up to you, isn't it? But if you don't, you'll never know what you're missing, will you?'

'No, I won't, will I?' I said, imitating his Welsh lilt.

His eyes glinted in the moonlight. 'Now you're imitating me, Claire Courtney . . . taking me off. . . ' Now he accentuated his own musical Welsh accent. 'And there's only one punishment I can think of, girl . . . '

With a squeal, I ran away, laughing as he chased after me. He gave me a ten-yard start, but I hadn't gone very far before he caught up with me. He gripped me round my waist and spun me round. The gleam of the river merged with the blanched trees. I pleaded to be let down, though when he did I was so giddy I had to cling to him.

'And now for the punishment,' he said, bringing his head down and kissing me.

When he'd finished, I looked up at him and smiled. 'There's lovely punishment, look you . . . I'd like some more, please, indeed to goodness . . . '

'Idiot!' he said, and laughing, let me go. 'We haven't spoken like that for years . . . '

We all met at the bus stop in the market square at eight o'clock the next morning, buzzing with excitement, and ready for the first stage of the journey to Cardiff. It seemed that everyone had put on their warmest clothes and Rhiannon was wearing her expensive sheepskin coat again.

Everyone seemed to be sporting red and white bobble caps and scarves. Gareth waved when he saw me. He had a huge red rosette on one lapel and an enormous plastic leek on the other. But though he didn't realize it, I too had an emblem.

Now for my defiant gesture, I thought as I approached. I stood in front of the small crowd and took a small paper Union Jack from behind my back.

'England for ever!' I yelled and waved it in the air.

There were cries of 'shame' and 'throw her in the river', and some of them made a dash for me. But Gareth reached me first.

'Hands off!' He ordered, thrusting me protectively behind him. 'This girl's got diplomatic immunity.'

I couldn't help noticing that Rhiannon was not amused.

I sat next to Elin on the bus, while Gareth and Steve sat behind us, singing Rugby songs, and before very long we arrived at Swansea to begin the half-mile trek to the railway station. It seemed that everyone else had had the same idea and I couldn't help wondering if British Rail had enough trains to take us to Cardiff.

Fortunately, they had provided a 'Rugby Special' in addition to their regular service, and though we had to stand, no one seemed to mind. There was an air of friendliness about – as though we were about to embark on a holiday.

The train arrived hours before the match was due to

begin so we girls decided to go window-shopping and we wandered from shop to shop enjoying ourselves thoroughly.

The hours flew and soon we were hurrying past the grey walls of Cardiff Castle to the large hotel where I'd arranged to meet Robert and Gareth. It dominated the street which led to the National Stadium and there at the door was Gareth. There was relief in his eyes when he saw me.

'Thought you were never coming,' he said, putting his arm through mine. 'We don't want to leave it too late . . . must get a decent place to watch the match.'

I was about to ask if he'd seen Robert when a hand tapped me on my shoulder and he was at my side.

'Hi, menace!' he said, his traditional greeting.

Gareth was the only one who had met him – and then only briefly the day that Robert had visited us – so I introduced him to Elin and Steve and the rest of the crowd. It was only then that I noticed Rhiannon.

'Oh, this is Rhiannon. I think I told you about her,' I said rather pointedly. 'Dad and Mr Evans work together . . . remember?'

Robert took her hand and shook it. 'Yes . . . of course I remember. Claire has told me a lot about you, Rhiannon, but . . . ' He flashed a provocative glance in my direction, ' . . . she never told me how attractive you were.'

To my amazement, Rhiannon actually blushed and the flush that came to her cheeks made her look even prettier. Then she simpered and looked up at him, and I knew that Robert had made one of his instant conquests.

There was a holiday feeling in the air as we pushed along the crowded street. On each side were stalls selling rosettes and scarves, ties and hats and badges of all description, and the aroma of hot-dogs and hamburgers wafted to us on the cool breeze. It was strange how many people seemed to know each other and the numerous cries of friendly greetings rang in my ears.

Suddenly, Gareth grabbed my hand and pulled me after him as he made for one of the stalls. He bought a papier mache bowler hat with a red dragon emblazoned on it and place it ceremoniously on my head.

'There. Nobody will ever guess you're English.'

I laughed, and together we weaved our way through the crowd until we were funnelled towards two enormous wrought-iron gates.

'Get behind me,' Gareth suggested. 'And stick close. I'll get us both inside in next to no time.'

I stuck to him like glue as he pushed and jostled his way past the barrier, his ticket prominently displayed in his right hand. Soon we were hurrying through a dark passage before running up some steps to emerge on to the East Terrace.

The first thing I noticed was the field, a brilliant emerald green in the cold and brittle sunlight. Already the ground seemed to be packed, though the numbers surging from all sides made me wonder how many more they'd be able to squeeze in. But squeeze them in they did; a friendly jovial crowd that burst into song as the brass band in the centre of the field played traditional airs and hymns.

A huge leek had already been pinned to one of the goalposts, while at the far end, a diminutive figure was being pursued by two burly policemen. There was a howl of friendly disapproval as he was caught and escorted back to the enclosure.

Eventually, the teams came out to be photographed

and an air of tension descended on the amphitheatre – broken only when the English team, dressed entirely in white, ran on to the field to the accompaniment of a modest clap.

But when the Welsh team emerged, resplendent in red and white, a deep roar emanated from all parts of the ground, a roar that grew and swelled and echoed into a deafening blast that made me put my hands over my ears. I felt my body break out in a rash of goose pimples as I was caught up in the infectious excitement.

Chapter 15

Though I don't think I would ever have admitted it to Gareth, I had never been a fanatical rugby supporter, but that game was one of the most thrilling matches I'd ever witnessed. It was a swift open game with plenty of excitement as the two sides attacked and defended with equal skill, so that at half-time, in spite of several near-tries that had all the spectators rising to their feet in the stands, there was no score.

It was the same in the second half and the play was so fast and strenuous that I wondered how the players managed to maintain the momentum. Tempers became frayed and at one time, the referee had to stop the game and warn both Welsh and English forwards against fighting.

Then about ten minutes before the end, the English backs broke through and their right-winger, tackled at the last moment by the full-back, went crashing over the line to score. A groan filled the stadium, only to become a relieved sigh a minute or two later when the English failed to convert.

The tension was like an electric current in a crowd that willed the Welsh team forward as it surged towards the English touchline. Three times they almost scored, only to be stopped at the last moment, and Gareth, who was hopping with frustration, told me that they were now into injury time. There were only seconds left in the game. Then, galvanized by the crowd, the Welsh left flanker, side-stepping neatly as he made a dummy pass, found an opening and went tearing for the line.

The people in front of me were jumping up and down in a frenzy and though I didn't see the try, I knew he had scored because of the roar that followed.

Then a hush of expectancy settled over the whole ground as the Welsh full-back, called upon by the captain, took the conversion kick.

If they converted, Wales would win.

Gareth couldn't bear to look. 'He can't miss . . . he mustn't . . .'

I had to smile at the sheer agony he was going through.

The full-back placed the ball carefully into the hollow he had made with the heel of his boot, stood in front of it for a moment, and then walked backwards. One, two, three, four, five, six, seven, eight, steps he took. Paused. Took a step to his left. Paused. Then ran forward and kicked. The ball soared into the air. Straight for the goalposts. Even as it left his foot, the crowd seemed to know that it was going straight and true. A swell rose from their throats.

But there was a stiff breeze that afternoon. It caught the ball which for a brief second seemed to hover in the air. Then it hit the left goalpost and was deflected behind the line. A sigh of disappointment breathed through the spectators.

The touch judges waved their flags close to the ground, and the referee blew his whistle for full time.

Gareth looked at me and grinned. 'You realize what's happened, don't you?' he said. 'We've both won.'

Then he put his arm round my shoulder and together we joined the surge towards the exit. As soon as we were out in the street, I wondered where Robert was.

'I said I'd see him before he went home,' I explained.

Elin gave me a nudge. 'Looks like he's busy,' and nodded to the other side of the road.

He and Rhiannon were talking. Then arm in arm, they walked away, and when we caught the train an hour or so later, Rhiannon wasn't with us.

Elin, Steve and I went back to Gareth's house where Mrs Morgan had arranged a supper for us. She heaped piles of chips on to plates already laden with bacon and eggs, and followed by large slabs of apple tart with ice-cream.

I decided later to phone my mother and asked her if Robert had arrived home.

'He got here about half-past six,' she told me. 'Not that he stayed long . . . we hardly had a chance to speak to him. And guess what? Who do you think he's taking out tonight? Rhiannon . . . Isn't that marvellous?'

Marvellous? Suddenly, I was angry. I felt betrayed – by my own brother – and I told him so at breakfast the next morning.

'I happen to think she's nice,' he protested. 'Not at all like the girl you once described to me . . . '

'Huh!' I poured myself a coffee. 'You would think that, wouldn't you? She'd naturally be nice to you. She'd be nice to anyone in trousers . . . '

Even as I uttered the words, I knew I was being unreasonably malicious.

Robert went quiet and I knew I had hurt him. 'You know as well as I do she's not a bit like that,' he said gravely. 'She's intelligent . . . and to be honest, I found her great company.'

I shrugged my shoulders. 'Perhaps she is. But don't you think she's a bit young for you?'

He leaned back in his chair and laughed. 'Come off it. I'm twenty and she's almost eighteen . . . just the right age difference I would have thought.'

I took a piece of toast and sullenly spread some marmalade on it. Neither of us spoke for a minute. Then Robert said, 'Look, Claire. I know things haven't been good between you two lately . . . but don't you think it's time to forget it all . . . I'm sure Rhiannon wants to . . . '

I didn't say anything. It was what I wanted, too, but at that moment I didn't know if I could.

Robert went down with a heavy cold later that day and couldn't return to university. Mum insisted that he stayed, declaring that he couldn't look after himself in a cold draughty bedsit and that he would recover much quicker if he stayed in a pleasant comfortable house and had warm nourishing meals. I could have told him it wasn't worth arguing. Mother always had her way.

Rhiannon tried to be friendly at school the next day. She approached me in the common room and began discussing the match which had been arranged with one of the Swansea Comprehensives the following Saturday and suggested we should get together and discuss tactics – as though nothing had ever happened between us.

I had by now decided that being friendly was perhaps by far the best policy and agreed. She gave a smile that seemed to harbour a certain sense of relief and arranged to see Miss Reynolds later that day to arrange a practice.

'By the way,' she said as she tagged along with Elin and me to the first lesson. 'How's Robert?'

Ah! I thought; now we're coming to the reason for all this amicability.

'All right.' I replied casually. 'Apart from his cold . . .'

She was immediately concerned. 'I didn't know he had a cold!'

'He didn't. Not on Saturday.'

I wasn't going to tell her he was still at home. Let Robert phone her and tell her himself, I thought, feeling vindictive.

But Elin had to go and tell her. 'That's why he didn't go back to university,' she said.

Predictably, Rhiannon called round that night. I had a feeling she would because earlier that day, she had borrowed my history notebook on the thinly veiled pretence of needing to catch up on some work she'd missed. I saw her walk coyly up the road and was waiting when the bell rang.

'I hope you don't mind me calling,' she said, glancing

hopefully over my shoulder. 'But I thought you might need your book . . .'

'Yes. I did as a matter of fact.' I deliberately kept her waiting in the porch. 'I thought I might do some revision.'

She gave a nervous smile. 'Just as well I brought it back then . . . How . . . how is Robert?'

'All right . . . I think.'

'Think?' There was just that tell-tale hint of disappointment in her voice. 'He hasn't gone back to university, has he?'

I intended keeping her in suspense but, a deep voice spoke from behind me. 'No, he hasn't gone back.'

It was Robert emerging far too soon for my liking from the lounge.

'Don't hang about, Rhiannon,' he said. 'Come in.'

I've never seen anyone move so fast in all my life. Before I could even move out of the way, she was past me, her face beaming with pleasure.

'Well, close the door, dear little sister.' Robert gave me a pinch that made me yell. 'You'll have me catch my death, if you're not careful.' He turned to Rhiannon and jerked his head in the direction of the kitchen. 'Come on. Let's make some coffee.'

They walked down the hall and I could hear Rhiannon saying how much she had enjoyed last Saturday and how she had come round as soon as she'd heard he was ill and how glad she was to see him slightly better. The words came out in a rush.

Both had forgotten about me, but I still remembered the times she'd tagged along with me and Gareth and decided it was time to have my own back. Robert was filling the kettle with water.

'Let me do that.' I took the kettle and plugged it in.

'Why don't you sit down with Rhiannon. You know how weak you're feeling, dear brother . . . '

Rhiannon glanced at us both with a perplexed frown on her forehead. 'Take no notice of her,' Robert said with a grin. 'She's always been protective towards me. And since you're on your feet, Claire, how about getting us some of that fruitcake Mum made yesterday?'

When Rhiannon told him not to bother, he quelled her protest. 'It's not a bother, is it, Claire? You like doing things for me . . . '

I just managed to curb my temper. 'Of course I do,' I replied, and banged the plates on the table. Rhiannon jumped.

There was an awkward silence as I made the coffee and when I set the tray down and sat opposite them, Rhiannon gave me a nervous smile. Robert looked across at me.

'I thought you said you had work to do,' he said pointedly.

I shrugged my shoulders. 'There's plenty of time. Anyway, how can I be so rude as to leave Rhiannon when she was kind enough to return my books to me?'

So Robert adopted a different strategy. He decided to ignore me.

He turned to Rhiannon. 'Would you like to come to Swansea again this Saturday?' he asked.

She opened her mouth to reply but I got in first.

'That will be wonderful,' I said. 'Thanks.'

He looked at me and frowned. 'I don't seem to remember asking you.'

I put on my most innocent expression. 'Oh, didn't you? I'm sorry . . . I thought you were talking to both of us . . . '

'Well, I . . . '

I knew what he was going to say and got in fast, again. 'You don't mind? That's great . . . and I assume I can ask Gareth as well.'

This wasn't what he expected and it showed. 'No!' he said awkwardly, glancing at Rhiannon who was by now completely bewildered. 'I don't suppose so . . . '

'Then it's settled. I'll phone Gareth right away and let him know . . . ' I got to my feet. At the door, I turned.

'By the way, you won't mind either if Elin and Steve come too, will you? I'm sure that banger of yours can hold six.'

He hated anyone to refer to the car he loved as a 'banger'. He opened his mouth to shout at me, then thought better of it.

'Of course I don't mind,' he said and gave me a grim smile. 'Now why don't you go and leave us alone . . . '

I didn't really intend going to Swansea, but the more I thought of it, the more the prospect appealed to me. But that was five days before the vital match, and something was to happen on that hockey pitch that would alter the whole situation.

Chapter 16

Friday afternoon was the time when the whole of the fifth and sixth years were grouped together for games; swimming and life-saving classes at the local swimming pool, table tennis and squash at the sports centre, and rugby and hockey on the playing fields. But since we were playing one of the Swansea Comprehensive Schools in an important league match, the girls had been told that activities had been suspended so that they could be spectators.

We were all keyed up when Miss Reynolds came into the changing rooms and gave us a pep talk. 'All I expect you to do is play your best . . . and I don't have to tell you, play clean . . . '

I wondered why she always said she didn't have to tell us and then went ahead and did so.

'You've all practised hard this week . . . so go out there, remember what I've told you, and play well.' She stood aside and opened the door.

There was a cheer from the spectators who were strung out along the side lines, and even the boys who were on the adjacent rugby pitch yelled their encouragement – including some remarks which were not quite so encouraging or complimentary.

Rhiannon spun a coin and gave the visiting captain the call – which she won, deciding to play from east to west.

'Trust!' Rhiannon muttered as we took up our positions. 'That means we'll have the sun in our eyes in the second half.'

There was nothing to do but play extra hard in the first half and build up a good score to make up for the disadvantage. The practices really did pay off and though the other side had the reputation of being the strong side, Rhiannon, Elin and I managed to score four goals between us in the first quarter of an hour. We played well together; with Elin on Rhiannon's left and me on her right and Jane backing us up, our tactics were working well. We were fed the right balls, placed in the right place at the right speed, with fast accurate passing. Several times, one of us was unmarked in the striking circle and it was only the skill and courage of their goalkeeper that prevented a higher score.

But then they rallied, and pushing well into our half, they put so much pressure on our defence that by half-time, they too had put in four goals.

Rhiannon gathered us round her during the break. 'Look, girls.' Like the rest of us she was breathing hard. 'We're going to be up against it in this half . . . ' She glanced at the sun which was now well down in the sky. 'Keep pushing the ball well up . . . make sure your passing's accurate . . . and whatever you do, try to keep them out of the striking circle . . . '

Miss Reynolds called us to our positions and we bullied-off. To begin with, everyone really did play hard, passing with such accuracy and determination that we were able to keep the play just where we wanted it. But gradually, they wore us down and after about ten minutes, they scored a lucky fifth goal – and shortly afterwards, a sixth and a seventh. I felt the determination drain out of my body.

Our play went haywire, and a few minutes later, disaster struck again. They burst through our defence and the ball went streaking to the right-wing who passed it expertly to the centre-forward. She had only the goalkeeper to beat. The sun had disappeared behind a thin band of cloud which had come in from the west, but just at the most vital moment, a momentary gleam dazzled our keeper.

Their centre-forward struck and the ball was once more in the net. Eight – four.

As we walked dejectedly back, Rhiannon rallied us

round. 'Come on, girls. We can't let them beat us . . . '

Where we got the energy from, I'll never know; but in the next fifteen minutes or so, we scored three times and brought the score to eight – seven.

It was one to draw or two to win.

We went for the win.

Within a minute, I was unmarked again in the striking area. Elin saw me, flicked the ball towards me – a perfect pass. I didn't hesitate. I scooped it up and slammed it into the net. The keeper didn't stand a chance.

I didn't know whether to laugh or cry with delight, and the sight of Robert and Gareth standing on the sideline, waving and cheering, made me feel elated.

'We can do it, Claire.' Elin was jubilant as we ran back together. 'Just one more . . . and we've won . . . '

We were now in the last minutes of the game with the visiting team more determined than ever. Miss Reynolds was glancing at her watch.

In the final bully-off, Rhiannon gained possession of the ball and sent it whizzing to the left-wing who was streaking away. Within seconds, we were in their twenty-five again, with Jane joining us once more in the attack. Again I was left unmarked. I couldn't believe that the strategy was working again in so short a time.

The ball was at my feet, but this time I was too slow. Their centre half, falling back, came swiftly into defence together with the right-back. There was a frantic mêlée in front of the goalmouth with Elin and Rhiannon joining in.

But then came disaster. I was wrongly placed, my stick was upright and the ball at my right foot; there were so many players around I couldn't move back.

I saw, as if in slow motion, Rhiannon's stick come across, lunging at the ball and missing. But it didn't miss me; it struck my foot.

The pain shot up my leg and burst right inside my head. For a moment, I was blinded. I fell to the ground, tears streaming down my cheeks, the nausea of stabbing pain in my throat. I heard the shouts from the side-line and, as though from a distance, a whistle blew.

I didn't understand that the ball had gone over the goal line or that the game was over. All I could think of was that Rhiannon had struck me. That it had been deliberate. That at last she'd had her revenge.

Gradually, I became aware that there were people crowding round, among them Elin and Rhiannon. I saw her through my tears. And as she knelt down beside me, all my anger spilled out.

'Don't touch me!' I thrust her away. 'Leave me alone! You're horrible. Just because Gareth . . . ' I gritted my teeth as spasms stabbed at my foot. 'Just because he prefers me.'

Perhaps because there was an element of truth in what I said, guilt and shame flooded her eyes.

Her face went white and she glanced round at the embarrassed stares from the other girls. Then she turned and pushed her way through the crowd of players.

Miss Reynolds came bursting through. 'All right, Claire. Don't move . . . ' She felt my foot and ankle, making me wince even though her touch was gentle. Her eyes were serious. 'I think we'd better get you to hospital, my girl . . . I think an X-ray is called for.'

By now Robert was at her side.

'I'll take her,' Robert said, adding when Miss

Reynolds objected. 'I'm her brother. And my car is parked on the road. So if someone could give me a hand . . .'

Within minutes, I was lying on the back seat, while Elin, who had volunteered to accompany us, sat next to Robert. As we drove away, I saw Gareth's anxious face at the window, and as we passed under the footbridge, saw Rhiannon running across in tears.

We were over two hours at the hospital. We had to wait for the result of the X-rays before leaving, and as I sat there, waiting impatiently with the pain now a dull throb, I felt bitterness surge inside me.

'That Rhiannon,' I said to Elin, gritting my teeth. Robert had gone to phone my mother and park the car in a more convenient spot. 'I hate her. You saw what she did . . . she deliberately struck me . . . just to get her own back.'

There was another stab of pain and I broke off, biting my lip.

Elin looked up, her eyes troubled.

'You're wrong, Claire. She didn't . . .'

I flashed her an angry glance. 'What are you talking about? I saw her.'

Elin looked down. 'So did I,' she said quietly. 'I was there. I just know it was an accident.'

I remembered the shame in Rhiannon's eyes when I accused her and the hurt when she ran away. Could I have been wrong? I wondered. Suddenly, I had doubts, because I knew that Elin would never lie to me.

'Are you sure?' I asked. 'Really sure?'

I knew what the answer was before she told me.

I gave a deep sigh. Through no one's fault but my own, the situation was getting worse. Indeed, the only good news was that my father's firm had reached an agreement with the unions that the only redundancies would be voluntary ones, so that the jobs of people like Turner's father were secure after all.

Chapter 17

I arrived home from hospital to a mother who fussed over a foot that, after all, had merely been badly bruised. Sitting in front of the television, I moaned about the fact that I wouldn't be able to go to Swansea with Robert the following evening or even to the town disco until the swelling had gone down. Thanks to Rhiannon, I said bitterly to myself. In spite of what Elin had said, I hadn't forgiven her.

So Robert made the suggestion that I should have a party at home instead and invite as many of my friends round as I wanted.

'Better than nothing,' he pointed out.

My mother had been only too happy to agree. 'We did say that the lounge was just the place for one,' she reminded me. 'As for food, the freezer's just been stocked. All we'll need to get is the drink. Your father can buy the coke tomorrow . . . '

'Coke? I couldn't ask my friends to drink Coke. They're not kids, Mum.'

'We could add Bacardi to it,' Robert suggested with a grin.

'No we won't.' My mother gave him a haughty

don't-encourage-her look. 'We'll have shandies instead.'

I gave another howl of protest. 'Oh, Mum! They all drink lager or beer . . . '

She gave me a frigid glance. 'Oh do they? If I'd known that I wouldn't have let you go out with them. I'll have to give that young man of yours a bit of my mind . . . '

I sat up and sent pain searing through my foot. 'Don't you dare. I'd be too ashamed to speak to him again.'

It was Robert who came to my rescue. 'It'll be all right. I'll take charge of the bar. I'll make sure no one drinks too much.' And gave me a broad wink.

So it was agreed that we'd have a party the following night and that I should phone my friends that very evening. So, after making a list of the people I wanted to invite, the receiver was plugged into a socket in the wall behind me.

'There's one more thing,' I said as I was about to dial. 'I don't want you or Dad in the house when the party's going on . . . '

My mother raised her eyebrows. 'So it's orders now! Then let me tell you this. I wouldn't dream of being here . . . as it happens your father and I have already arranged to go out with Rhiannon's parents . . . '

I breathed a sigh of relief and started dialling. One by one, I worked through the list: Elin, Steve, Jane . . . all of them were only too glad to have a Saturday night out where all the food and drinks were free.

I left Rhiannon till last, and asked Robert if he would prefer to ask her.

He shook his head. 'It's your party. I think you should invite her. Just say that the trip to Swansea is off and that I'll phone her tomorrow.'

Glad now of the chance of preventing Robert from hearing how I'd humiliated her at the hockey match, I dialled her number, though I waited until he was out of the room first.

It was her mother who came to the phone. 'I'm afraid she's not in at the moment . . .' she said. I detected a hint of coldness in her voice; or was it my guilty conscience, I wondered. 'I'll get her to phone you later if that's all right . . .'

But she never phoned back – not even the following morning – and it angered me so much at the time that I was determined not to bow down and beg her to come. I'd made my move; the next was up to her.

Later that day, Robert came from the phone with a worried frown on his forehead. 'I've been trying to get in touch with Rhiannon,' he said. 'Her mother says she's not in . . .and that's the third time I've tried. You did phone her last night, didn't you?'

'Of course I did.' I wasn't exactly lying, but I wasn't telling the truth either.

He shook his head and went back to watch his sports programme on television.

By eight o'clock, almost everybody had arrived – except Rhiannon, Elin and Steve. Mum had laid out a table along one wall and covered it with food: sausage rolls, sandwiches, crisps, cheese and pickles, several quiches, some plates containing portions of pizza and three large gateaux. At the other end, Robert had constructed a makeshift bar and was busy dispensing drinks. I saw him glance at his watch several times. Gareth had volunteered to be in charge of the music centre and since we'd pushed everything to the walls, there was plenty of room for dancing.

The doorbell rang and as I hobbled out to answer it, Robert followed me. As I expected, Elin and Steve had arrived.

Predictably, there was no sign of Rhiannon, and it was obvious that she wouldn't be turning up. The realization made me feel guilty.

Robert put his arm on my shoulder after I'd shown Steven and Elin into the lounge and kept me in the hall. 'You did say you'd spoken to Rhiannon, didn't you?'

'Well . . . ' I began. 'Not exactly . . . '

'What do you mean? Not exactly?'

There was a glint of suspicion in his eyes that made me feel ashamed.

'I didn't exactly speak to her. It was her mother who answered the phone . . . '

'Why didn't you tell me?' His eyes were now hard and accusing. 'You knew I was worried when I couldn't get in touch with her . . . '

'I didn't think it was important.' Now I was lying.

'Not important? Come off it, Claire.' He broke off and his suspicion hardened. 'She ran off the field yesterday after the accident.' He turned back to me. 'Right. I want to know the truth. I want to know what happened between you two . . . '

When Robert was in that determined mood, I knew better than to lie. So I told him everything – not that there was really much to say. He made no comment, but his expression told me exactly what he thought of me.

'You realize that what you've done is as bad as anything she's done?' He waved aside my protests.

'It's no use trying to make excuses. You knew I was keen on her . . . yet you deliberately lied to me.'

I bowed my head. 'I know . . . I'm sorry.'

But he was far from placated. 'Being sorry's not enough. I want to know what you're going to do about it.'

'What can I do?' I wailed.

'You can get her here . . . that's what you can do.'

I looked up at him. 'You mean phone?'

He shook his head angrily and snorted. 'No, I don't mean phone. You're coming with me to her house . . . and you're going to apologize.'

I moved away from him. 'But my foot . . . '

'To hell with your foot. You can get about on it if you want to. Now . . . !' He went to the cloakroom and flung my jacket at me. 'Do I have to carry you to my car? Or are you going to walk?'

He drove like a madman, hunched over the steering-wheel and staring grimly in front of him. Within minutes, we had pulled up outside Rhiannon's house. He switched off the engine and turned to me. Some of his anger had dissipated.

'It seems to me, Claire,' he said slowly, evenly. 'That you both have a lot of apologizing to do, and though you may think it is all her fault . . . and you may be right . . . I think you should make the first move?'

I looked at him apprehensively.

'Look!' His voice was gentle now. 'I don't expect you to go on your hands and knees, but I would like you to make it plain that you'd like her to come to the party. Please, Claire . . . for me . . . '

I couldn't speak. All I could do was gulp hard and nod.

We had to ring four times before we saw, through the thickly patterned glass of the front door, a dim shape coming down the stairs. The door opened slightly and Rhiannon appeared.

'Hi!' It was Robert who spoke first. 'Can we see you

a minute?'

For a moment, I thought she was going to slam the door in our faces, and Robert, who must have suspected it too, thrust his foot in the doorway.

'Please, Rhiannon . . we've come to see how you are. Please let us in . . .'

Reluctantly, she stepped back and allowed us into the hall. Her eyes were red and puffy and she seemed too embarrassed to look at us. Robert nudged me.

'I want . . .' I hesitated, conjuring up the right words. 'I want to say I'm sorry . . . for what happened yesterday . . . and . . . and I'd like you to come to the party . . .'

'We'd both like you to,' he added quietly.

She glanced at him and a smile flickered on her lips. When she spoke, her voice was hoarse.

'But I can't . . . not like this . . . I'm not ready.'

'That's all right.' Robert's voice was gentle but determined. 'We can wait. Can't we, Claire?'

I nodded. 'Yes . . . yes of course we can.'

I thought she was going to refuse, but then Robert said, 'Come on, Rhiannon. We'll have a fantastic time.'

It was twenty minutes later when she came down the stairs and joined us in the living-room.

She had washed and changed, brushed her hair so that it gleamed like burnished gold in the light, and by the skilful use of make-up, had hidden the red rims around the eyes that so much crying had caused. But at the door she hesitated once more and held back, so that I thought we were going to go through the act of persuasion again. But what she had to say surprised both of us.

'Before we go, I think you ought to know something . . . especially you, Robert . . .' She paused for a second before going on. 'I don't know if Claire has told you . . . about my being bitchy towards her, but it's true. I did try to make things difficult . . . turning the girls against her . . . making her look a fool. But that was because . . . well, it doesn't matter . . . not any more . . .' Then she turned to me. 'But what happened yesterday . . . that was an accident . . . it really was. Please, you must believe me . . .'

I looked at Robert, then at Rhiannon. Tears were stinging my eyes and I wanted to kick myself for behaving so ridiculously.

'But I do believe you,' I said, my throat feeling so tight that the words wouldn't come out properly. I turned away and opened the door. 'I think we ought to forget all that has happened, don't you?'

Robert drove back at a much more respectable speed. Rhiannon sat next to him, while I was relegated to the back seat – where I belonged. As they spoke to each other, Rhiannon's eyes shining now as she gazed across at him, I was totally ignored.

Not that I minded. It gave me a chance to think of Gareth and school and the rest of the girls. As I did so, I realized with an increasing sense of joy that the future was going to be so different.

My father's job hopefully would be less difficult, my mother would open her boutique and live a full life again, and perhaps, seeing that Robert had an incentive for coming home, we'd see a lot more of him. But more than anything, I had the notion that Rhiannon and I would become even closer friends.

I sat back as we pulled into the drive and sighed with happiness. Robert had been so right. There was a time for forgetting; there was a time for forgiving.

And this was it.

Fiction

☐	**The Chains of Fate**	Pamela Belle	£2.95p
☐	**Options**	Freda Bright	£1.50p
☐	**The Thirty-nine Steps**	John Buchan	£1.50p
☐	**Secret of Blackoaks**	Ashley Carter	£1.50p
☐	**Lovers and Gamblers**	Jackie Collins	£2.50p
☐	**My Cousin Rachel**	Daphne du Maurier	£2.50p
☐	**Flashman and the Redskins**	George Macdonald Fraser	£1.95p
☐	**The Moneychangers**	Arthur Hailey	£2.95p
☐	**Secrets**	Unity Hall	£2.50p
☐	**The Eagle Has Landed**	Jack Higgins	£1.95p
☐	**Sins of the Fathers**	Susan Howatch	£3.50p
☐	**Smiley's People**	John le Carré	£2.50p
☐	**To Kill a Mockingbird**	Harper Lee	£1.95p
☐	**Ghosts**	Ed McBain	£1.75p
☐	**The Silent People**	Walter Macken	£2.50p
☐	**Gone with the Wind**	Margaret Mitchell	£3.95p
☐	**Wilt**	Tom Sharpe	£1.95p
☐	**Rage of Angels**	Sidney Sheldon	£2.50p
☐	**The Unborn**	David Shobin	£1.50p
☐	**A Town Like Alice**	Nevile Shute	£2.50p
☐	**Gorky Park**	Martin Cruz Smith	£2.50p
☐	**A Falcon Flies**	Wilbur Smith	£2.50p
☐	**The Grapes of Wrath**	John Steinbeck	£2.50p
☐	**The Deep Well at Noon**	Jessica Stirling	£2.95p
☐	**The Ironmaster**	Jean Stubbs	£1.75p
☐	**The Music Makers**	E. V. Thompson	£2.50p

Non-fiction

☐	**The First Christian**	Karen Armstrong	£2.50p
☐	**Pregnancy**	Gordon Bourne	£3.95p
☐	**The Law is an Ass**	Gyles Brandreth	£1.75p
☐	**The 35mm Photographer's Handbook**	Julian Calder and John Garrett	£6.50p
☐	**London at its Best**	Hunter Davies	£2.90p
☐	**Back from the Brink**	Michael Edwardes	£2.95p

☐ Travellers' Britain	} Arthur Eperon	£2.95p
☐ Travellers' Italy		£2.95p
☐ The Complete Calorie Counter	Eileen Fowler	90p
☐ The Diary of Anne Frank	Anne Frank	£1.75p
☐ And the Walls Came Tumbling Down	Jack Fishman	£1.95p
☐ Linda Goodman's Sun Signs	Linda Goodman	£2.95p
☐ The Last Place on Earth	Roland Huntford	£3.95p
☐ Victoria RI	Elizabeth Longford	£4.95p
☐ Book of Worries	Robert Morley	£1.50p
☐ Airport International	Brian Moynahan	£1.95p
☐ Pan Book of Card Games	Hubert Phillips	£1.95p
☐ Keep Taking the Tabloids	Fritz Spiegl	£1.75p
☐ An Unfinished History of the World	Hugh Thomas	£3.95p
☐ The Baby and Child Book	Penny and Andrew Stanway	£4.95p
☐ The Third Wave	Alvin Toffler	£2.95p
☐ Pauper's Paris	Miles Turner	£2.50p
☐ The Psychic Detectives	Colin Wilson	£2.50p

All these books are available at your local bookshop or newsagent, or
can be ordered direct from the publisher. Indicate the number of copies
required and fill in the form below   12

....

Name_____
(Block letters please)

Address_____

_____

Send to CS Department, Pan Books Ltd, PO Box 40, Basingstoke, Hants
Please enclose remittance to the value of the cover price plus:
35p for the first book plus 15p per copy for each additional book ordered
to a maximum charge of £1.25 to cover postage and packing
Applicable only in the UK

While every effort is made to keep prices low, it is sometimes
necessary to increase prices at short notice. Pan Books reserve
the right to show on covers and charge new retail prices which
may differ from those advertised in the text or elsewhere